Three Dimensions of Learning

Three Dimensions of Learning

A Blueprint for Learning
from the Womb to the School

Dr. Carolyn Nooks Teague

ARCHWAY
PUBLISHING

Archway Publishing books may be ordered through booksellers or by contacting:

Archway Publishing
1663 Liberty Drive
Bloomington, IN 47403
www.archwaypublishing.com
1 (888) 242-5904

ISBN: 978-1-4808-5274-7 (sc)
ISBN: 978-1-4808-5275-4 (hc)
ISBN: 978-1-4808-5276-1 (e)

Library of Congress Control Number: 2017916295

Print information available on the last page.

Archway Publishing rev. date: 11/28/2017

CONTENTS

PREFACE

IT IS NOW THE WINTER OF 2015, AND I AM BEING guided by God to share what I have learned as a parent, teacher, doctor of education, and Christian about teaching and learning as it occurs in the womb, the home, and the school.

I represent the unheard voices of the silent majority who have a vested interest in the future of our children but little to no say about their education.

I dedicate this book to my mother, Gladys Pennie-Nooks Reed, my role model, who was an elementary teacher and taught me to be patient, compassionate, and resilient, my husband, Will Teague Jr., who supported me through all my endeavors and extra years of education, also to my children, Lauren Teague Payne and Will Ryan Teague, who taught me the true meaning of unconditional love and are the lights of my life, my sister, Angela Nooks Byrd, who was and still is always there for me, my niece and nephew, Ashara and Joe Brockhaus for technical support and last but not least, Salvatore Zabbatino, who was so instrumental in helping me with the technology involved in earning a doctoral degree in education.

My love and compassion for the whole child's overall development is the catalyst that inspires this work. The resistance of college professors of education and scientists to be informed by one another is what saddens and frustrates me, and the dedication of our teachers, in spite of having to work in an atmosphere of political greed, ignorance, and misguided visions, is what drives me to write this book.

INTRODUCTION

Perspectives of the Silent Majority: How Did We End Up Here?

A S ADULTS, WE ARE ALL RESPONSIBLE FOR OUR futures, and developing the children that will become our leaders is part of that responsibility. As parents, our roles are crucial, for learning begins in the womb and continues in the home, so what we do as caregivers to prepare—or maybe not prepare—our children for life in general, and school in particular, determines the future of us all.

As teachers and educators, it is our responsibility to love children unconditionally, regardless of race, religion, or ethnography, and accept them where they are academically and help them grow. It is our responsibility to seek knowledge about the child's physical, mental, and emotional development and how the many facets of each child are all interconnected. As university department heads, it is your responsibility to be objective as well as open to new research-based science that could possibly inform and even reform educational practices. It is your responsibility to be able to ensure future educators that what they are learning is cutting-edge information, which will impact the nature of education, even if only to a small degree. You must inform our future teachers about the importance of addressing the child's brain-body-spirit-connection and the need to reach the child at an emotional level. Every teacher needs to understand how the brain learns, how the body and brain connect, and most important, how emotions control it all. Being aware of and addressing the connectedness of the dimensions of the child is crucial to all who interact with children throughout the dimensions of learning.

Education is incomplete when it only addresses the linguistic and mathematical intelligences of the child. It becomes complete when it validates the whole child by giving him the opportunity to express his passions, develop additional intelligences and interests, and be made to feel valuable within a community of learners.

The three dimensions of learning to which I am referring intrinsically involve the connectedness of the child's brain, mind (spirit), and body development but specifically examine the development of the brain and how it impacts learning in the womb, the home, and the school. There is a fourth dimension, but that's another book.

Some of you have read books and articles about the science behind learning, written by medical doctors, cognitive psychologists, and college professors, but have you read anything from the classroom teacher or parent's perspective? Well, I am sharing information as a parent, a teacher, and a doctor of education with a strong interest in the science of learning. I am not a scientist; I'm just a parent and a teacher who is passionate about our children's lives.

I decided to write this book for the silent majority, composed of parents, teachers, and last but not least, children. I call these groups of people the silent majority because we have neither voice nor input into educational practices and programs, even though we are the ones most affected by their implementation or lack thereof.

In today's educational culture, all of the learning that takes place, from conception in the womb to graduation in the school, boils down to a child's test scores, not his moral development, creative genius, or social aptitude. "What did this child do to help our global educational rankings?" is the question that drives educational policies.

In spite of what we have learned in the last two decades about the way the brain develops and functions, the way children learn, and what environmental conditions provide for optimal learning, we seem to be going in the wrong direction. Legislators who know little about proper educational practices, driven by global educational rankings and the promises and prerequisites of political gain, make decisions about what's best for our children. The fear of not being first or at least in the top ten on academic success lists has landed us in the quagmire of testing frenzy. As a result, we teach to the test, not to the child.

You might be asking yourself, "What the heck does this testing frenzy have to do with the dimensions of learning? What does it have to do with the dimensional connectedness of the whole child, the brain, mind (spirit), emotions, and body?" It has everything to do with this connection and the role it plays in a supportive educational environment. It has everything to do with viewing the whole child instead of the part of that child that makes him or her a good candidate for test-taking. It has everything to do with how our curricula and educational programs should be designed and how our schools should reflect and be guided by acknowledging all dimensions of learning, as well as the dimensions of the child. Maybe educating the whole child could result in better test scores and higher rankings, since twenty years of what we have been doing, hasn't seemed to work. (Just saying.)

When children enter school for the first time, teachers begin the year with testing to see where children are academically. You know what I mean—kindergarten teachers need to assess children according to whether they know their colors, recognize the letters of the alphabet, can count to ten, and so forth. Some of these children have emotional meltdowns and so begin their futures in school on a negative note.

How many teachers actually take the time to learn about a different dimension of the child, one that is crucial to his or her academic success? How many teachers actually have the kind of time it takes to get to investigate the physical, social, spiritual, and emotional states of the child's being before the hardcore academics begin?

In their defense, teachers are underpaid and under pressure to follow strict guidelines. They are directed to do certain activities in the classroom that center on "core curricula." These activities do not provide the teacher with opportunities to learn and know the child in more than one dimension. In some instances, they are actually instructed to follow a script. Teachers, against their better judgment, have been ordered to take play time out of the daily schedule. They've been directed to decrease time for recess, and in some districts, to omit recess to replace it with instructional activities. In some schools, physical education and art have been removed to make more time for test preparation and increased academics. The emotional state of the child is obviously not taken into consideration.

What happened to the truly educated leaders who recognized the importance of social play, physical activity, and the arts in the education of our children? What happened to the voices of the educators who realized that education involves addressing the learning dimensions of the whole child? How did we get to a place where our children are merely statistics, vessels to be filled with information that will be regurgitated on high-stakes tests?

How did education become so punitive in nature? The students are punished for not scoring well on a test that does not make allowances for their particular learning style or dominant intelligence. A child's broken home life or undetected learning disability is never considered. The teachers are punished for the students' poor performances, and the administrators have to deal with the brunt of it all.

Learned, passionate educators are still out there. However, their voices cannot be heard against the loud roar of political machines that began with global prowess and the institution of high-stakes testing in 1995. Unfortunately, this entity, with a life of its own, has mindlessly progressed to the present with common core teaching and testing, and when this phase ends, another will take its place.

While educators and parents agree that some form of standardized assessment is necessary to measure how well children are learning and diagnose what they need, they disagree with an assessment system that is punitive. They want to replace testing that ignores the different learning styles and the learning strengths of all students. They realize that our present assessment system leaves no time for teachable moments or the construction of knowledge. They are frustrated by a system that causes stress for the students, parents, teachers, and administrators alike. They feel helpless in their struggle to make changes in the educational process that would be more compatible with how children develop mentally, socially, emotionally, physically, and spiritually.

I'm sure that most politicians want to do what's best for the people, but they lack knowledge and understanding of how children actually learn, so they do what they think is right, based on faulty, jaundiced information and data they receive.

As parents, once our children leave our domain, we don't always know what's academically best for them. We are not privy to research findings that color the school curricula. As teachers, we might be aware of what makes for sound educational policies, but we do not have the freedom to allow children to discover and construct their own knowledge. We do not have the power to determine what we will teach or how we will teach it. We do not have the time to figure out how each child is connected, mentally, physically, and spiritually or emotionally. We have to use valuable time testing constantly, collecting test data and recording and reporting this data to district administrators, who in turn collect and report data to the state department of education.

Maybe if we all understood the relevance of the way the brain develops and how the respective sequence and hierarchy of this development affects the connectedness of the whole child, we would design school programs and curricula to support and enhance them. We would provide tests that would be used to diagnose and strengthen them. Maybe then our children would do better in school and subsequently in life.

Figure P1 by Brenda Hunter

PART I

The First Dimension of Learning: The Journey Begins in the Womb with the Blueprint

CHAPTER 1

Learning and Development in the Womb: The Making of the Whole Child

*A*S WE BEGIN THIS JOURNEY, LET ME BE PER-*fectly clear. God has provided us with a blueprint for dealing with the whole child.* It's up to us to provide the proper construction. The hierarchy and sequence of development that He has put in place tells us what is important and necessary for the child's learning and development (Melillo, 2009).

Right now, whether you believe in God or not, I am talking to you, the parent, or soon-to-be parent, the educator, and the politician, who need to understand more about how an infant develops into a whole child. For some of you this information might be redundant, but I have to cite myself as an example of an educated dummy. I considered myself to be fairly intelligent. I attended a school for the gifted, graduated from college, and earned a master's degree, then a doctorate in education. In spite of all of these accomplishments, I remained very ignorant; I didn't know jack about our children's cognitive, sensory, or emotional development in the womb, things so important that they actually have a major impact on a child's future.

Due to advances in technology, what scientists have learned over the last twenty years is mind-boggling. What they now know is incredibly important and informative about the development of that tiny life that will one day be an independent adult. Even before a woman realizes she is pregnant, a new life has taken form and is developing and being influenced by everything she does, as well as everything that happens around her in her environment.

We are all aware of the physical growth and development of the baby inside the womb because it's something we can actually see occurring. We watch in awe as the mother's stomach expands with the size of the fetus, and we respond to this by being considerate, offering expectant mothers a seat by giving up our own, and the kind, considerate gestures go on and on.

But how many of us are really thinking about the development of the baby's brain and sensory organs? How many of us actually consider that the fetus has an emotional state? I know I didn't give this very much thought, if any. The baby's physical development, while crucial, is not as sensitive to environmental factors as the developing brain. Genes contribute about 60 percent of brain development, environment in the uterus about 30 percent, and the mother's nutrition about 10 percent. So, while most of the brain's development is based on genetics, sound, healthy development depends on certain external factors that need to be addressed and/or avoided. How do we all respond to this unobservable development? Usually, we don't respond with any intentional good deeds to give the mother comfort or support for the baby's developing brain. Do we even know what matters? Understanding brain development in the fetus should actually take precedence over physical development because all of the progress as well as regression in our lives can be attributed to how our brains work. I sure wish I had known more of this. Thank God I didn't have any bad habits; my children are wonderful. There's no telling how they could have turned out had I been a smoker, druggie, or alcoholic. I'm just saying.

Let's begin with a very basic timeline of fetal development with emphasis on brain development. This timeline is divided into trimesters, which divides the pregnancy into thirds (Surebaby.com, 2016).

The First Trimester

Week 1–2: The egg gets implanted into the wall of the uterus. Conception is completed, and the age of the embryo begins at two weeks.

Week 3: The backbone, heart, blood vessels, and brain begin to form.

Week 4: The three brain sections—the forebrain, middle brain, hind brain—and optical stalk develop. Your baby becomes an embryo.

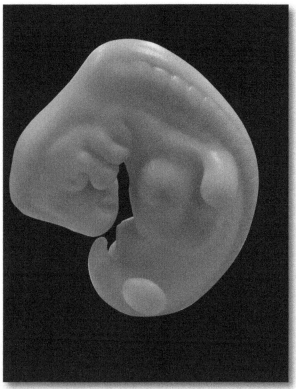

Figure 1.1 At four weeks, the fertilized egg becomes an embryo. It is as big as a poppy seed.

Week 5: The brain continues to develop and control the circulatory system with four chambers of the heart functioning.

Week 6–7: The two hemispheres of the brain form, and the neural tube that connects the brain and the spinal cord closes. The brain grows rapidly. Your baby is now called a fetus.

Week 8: The development of the hind brain, responsible for breathing, regulating heart beat and correlated muscle movements begins.

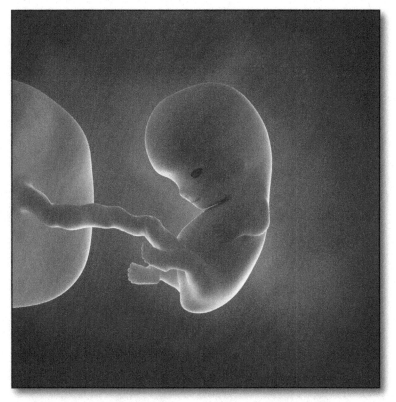

Figure 1.2 By week nine, the embryo is officially a fetus.
It is the size of a kidney bean.

Week 9: The nervous system is developed enough for proper functioning.

Week 10: The brain is forming 250,000 neurons (brain cells) per minute. The fetus is the size of a large strawberry.

Week 11: Spinal nerves start to branch out from the clearly defined spinal cord. Miniature ovaries and testicles have finished forming.

Week 12: Brain growth slows down, and taste buds and vocal cords develop.

Week twelve marks the end of the first trimester. Just three months have passed, but an amazing amount of development has occurred. The possibility of miscarriage has decreased.

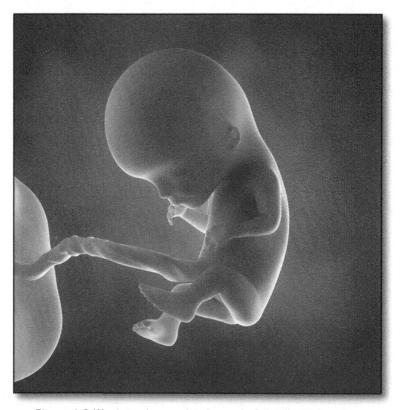

Figure 1.3 Week twelve marks the end of the first trimester. Before the "baby bump" is even obvious, God's amazing creation has taken on the persona of a real human being.

The Second Trimester:

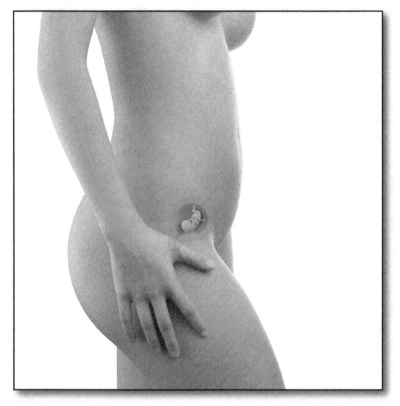

Figure 1.4 Fetus pictured in womb at end of first trimester.
The fetus is about the size of a lime.

Week 13: End of first trimester, brain has put the heart, liver, spleen, and many other organs to work.

Week 14: The brain starts the inhaling and exhaling function.

Week 15: The sense of hearing increases at this stage.

Week 16: Movement in the form of tugging on the umbilical cord is occurring.

Figure 1.5 At week sixteen, baby reaches for and tugs on umbilical cord. The fetus is the size of an avocado.

Week 17: The spinal cord develops a protective barrier of tough material called myelin around itself, the uterus is expanding, and bones are growing and getting hard.

Week 18: The brain is growing rapidly; the baby develops sensitivity to light.

Week 19: The brain forms millions of motor neurons, enabling the fetus to make voluntary movement. The forebrain morphs into the left and right hemispheres. The nerve cells required for the functions of all the senses are developing rapidly.

Week 20: Nerve cells are making complex connections involving sensory perception with the brain and the entire body.

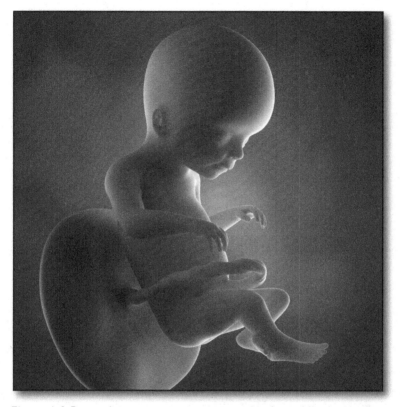

Figure 1.6 By week twenty, sensory perception is rapidly developing. The fetus is about the size of a large banana.

Week 21: Growth of the fetus slows down while the heart gets stronger and fat accumulates in the baby's muscles.

Week 22: The brain is translating complex sensory perceptions, and the fetus begins to distinguish between different sounds.

Week 23: All the nerve cells that developed independently migrate together to form a complete nervous system.

Week 24: The brain starts to regulate all body functions and activates the auditory and visual systems, which heightens the baby's overall senses.

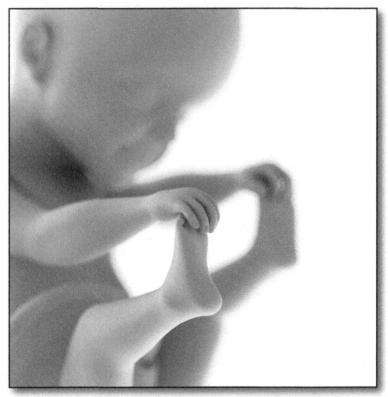

Figure 1.7 The brain now regulates all body functions.
Auditory and visual systems are activated.
The fetus is about the size of a large ear of corn.

Week 25: The nervous system is now developed enough to control voluntary breathing, the spinal cord begins to stiffen and straighten out, and the optic nerve perceives light from any direction.

Week 26: The surface of the brain begins to change from smooth to creased and wavy. Visual and auditory senses are enhanced as brain waves get stronger.

Week 27: Brain tissues are developing at a rapid rate while the brain is actively processing many senses. At this point, the baby begins to dream, and emotions in dreams are observable (facial expressions).

Week 28: The brain is in complete control of breathing and monitoring body temperature as it continues to develop more creases and fissures.

Week twenty-eight marks the end of the second trimester, and with the exception of vision, the sensory-motor connections of the whole child are in place.

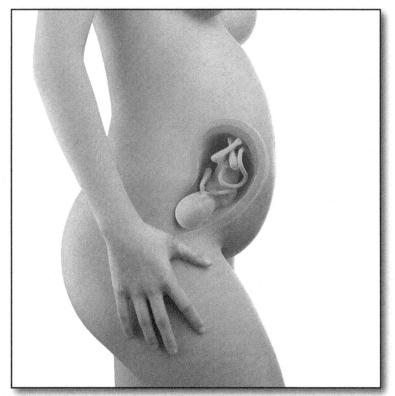

Figure 1.8 Twenty-eight weeks marks the end of the second trimester. The fetus is about the size of a butternut squash.

The Third Trimester

Figure 1.9 Rapid brain growth along with development
of the lungs occur during the third trimester.
The fetus is now the size of a large watermelon.

Weeks 29–40: The brain continues to grow rapidly while forming millions of synapses and connections along with the lungs, which is the last organ to develop, close to the end of the third trimester. At birth the infant brain is only one-fourth the size of the adult brain. (Rajeev, 2012)

As I continue, I hope you are realizing that all of these different areas of development, while they have their own sequence, are developing simultaneously, forming the whole child.

It's important to realize that God has provided us with a blueprint of how to address the needs of the developing child. He has shown us through modern science what the hierarchy and sequence of development is. Now it's up to us to make sense of this information and use it to benefit future generations.

CHAPTER 2

Taking a Closer Look at Brain Development: A Blueprint for Learning

*T*HE FETAL NERVOUS SYSTEM, THE BABY'S BRAIN and spinal cord, make up one of the very first systems to develop. Once again, it is actually forming before you even know you are pregnant.

The brain develops in a specific sequence, from basic to complex parts (BabyCentre, 2016). Without getting too scientific, some interesting facts need to be presented. Think about this: just sixteen days after conception, the neural plate, which is the foundation of your baby's brain and spinal cord, are already forming. This neural plate grows and eventually ends up being the neural tube. Once this tube closes at about the sixth or seventh week of pregnancy, it bulges into three sections: the forebrain, midbrain, and hindbrain. Just to the rear of the hindbrain is the section that will develop into the spinal cord. Soon these areas curve and bulge in the five areas many of us are familiar with: the cerebrum, cerebellum, brain stem, hypothalamus, and pituitary gland. At the same time, millions of neural cells form and migrate throughout the embryo, connecting to millions of other cells to form the baby's nervous system. With the connections of these neural cells, movement begins in the fetus way before you can feel it. At about eight weeks, your baby is able to wiggle limbs. At the end of the first trimester, twelve weeks, your baby is not only able to move limbs but also develops the sense of touch, and I repeat, you're probably not even showing.

With a functioning simple brain in operation, the baby begins to practice breathing, and the first sucking and swallowing impulses kick in. By twenty-one weeks, breathing and tasting amniotic fluid are in full gear. At twenty-four weeks, a huge reflex, blinking, occurs, and the continuing development of the brainstem, which controls heart rate, breathing, and blood pressure, is almost mature. The baby's nervous system has developed enough for your baby to be startled by loud noises outside the womb. The baby even turns his head to the sound of your voice. At twenty-eight weeks, babies develop REM (rapid eye movement), which is indicative of dreaming (Hopson, J. L., 2016). Make sure you provide good dreams for your baby.

By the third trimester, the baby's brain triples in size, growing from about 3.5 ounces to 10.6 ounces at term. The brain's appearance changes from having a smooth surface to having a grooved, indented surface, which is indicative of the growth of more neurons and specialized brain activity.

At the same time, the *cerebellum*, which controls reflexive movement, is growing faster than any other area of the brain. No wonder you start to feel all those kicks and turning. While the *cerebral cortex,* the area of thinking, remembering and feeling, is also developing, it is not functional until the baby is born and continues to develop after birth. For some of us, the frontal lobes, the reasoning part of the cerebral cortex, seems to take at least twenty-one years to develop, probably even longer for some of us, not mentioning any sex, but just saying.

It is crucial to your baby's healthy development for you to have proper nutrition and eliminate smoking, alcohol, and any other toxins that can be harmful (Norman & Ludwin, 2008). Even if a woman is just trying to get pregnant, she should start the good habits early on. I know I'm repeating myself. Oh well, this stuff is important, and some of us have to be told something more than once for it to sink in or register as being significant.

There is a really scary misconception out there concerning the baby's well-being and when to start making lifestyle changes. I've actually heard expectant mothers say that they plan to stop smoking or drinking once they are three months pregnant; they have no idea what harm might have already been done by that time. I said all of this to emphasize that *waiting until after you know you're pregnant to make positive lifestyle changes is not good enough.*

Since scientists estimate that genes contribute about 60 percent of the brain's development while in the uterus, and the mother's nutrition and environmental exposures contribute the remaining 40 percent, then almost half of the input of the baby's development is dependent on what the mother does to her body and what she is exposed to in her daily life and routines. Let's be more specific about how this organ, the brain, is shaped by things other than genes.

Here's the thing—the development of your child's brain is affected by the interaction and influence of four major factors: *genes,* which you cannot control, *internal activities*/sleep, which you can try to control, *external* experiences and stimulation, which may or may not be under your control, and the *environment.*

The environment consists of four components, which, in my opinion, are mostly under your control: *the physical* environment (relating to space, position in space, movement, motor development, and the ability to move), the *chemical environment* (referring to nutrition as well as the exposure to toxic substances around us), the *sensory environment* (experiencing different types of sounds, voice, touch, smell, movement, and vision and sleep cycles, which are essential for the complete development of the nervous system), and the *social/emotional* environment (the characteristic that is attached to all sensory stimuli and provides for social/emotional learning and memory). Stop and think about how many of these things can be controlled by you, and remember that some of these factors will continue to affect development as your child grows and learns (Graven & Browne, 2008).

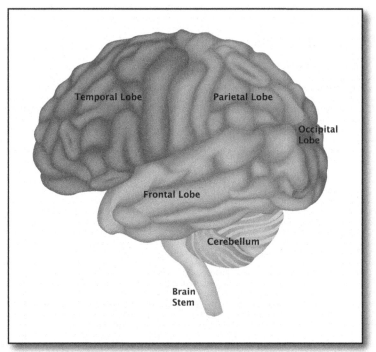

Figure 2.1 The brainstem develops first because it controls functions necessary for life.

As we look at the process of learning, we need to pay attention to the fact that the brain develops in a specific sequence, like everything else, from the most basic parts to the most complex. So you might ask, "Why is this so important?" Well, it's important because it shows us what's most important to the child's ability to perceive, retain, and retrieve information. The *brain stem,* along with the hypothalamus and pituitary, develop first, which makes sense, because together, they control the physical body. The brainstem controls basic functions like breathing and heart rate, while the hypothalamus regulates body homeostasis or stability, including thirst and hunger, and the pituitary gland is responsible for producing hormones. These functions are necessary for life and the physical condition of the child. This tells us that the child's physical condition plays a huge role in learning. How much is a child going to learn if all he or she can think about is being hungry? Thinking about food will take precedence over any information being presented.

The next part of the brain to develop is the *cerebellum*, which controls reflexive movement, motion control, balance and coordination, motor learning, and cognition, which show us that movement and learning go hand in hand.

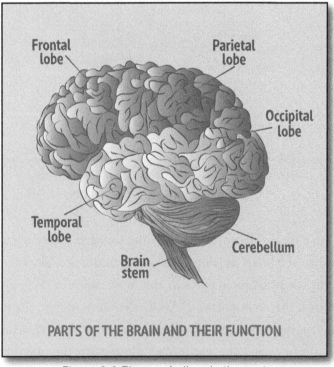

Figure 2.2 The cerebellum is the next
part of the brain to develop.

This part is followed by the *limbic system* (responsible for processing emotions and storing memories), and this speaks volumes to the role that this system plays in learning. If a child is emotionally engaged, having fun during learning experiences, his or her chances for retention are increased exponentially. The limbic system is just beneath the cerebrum.

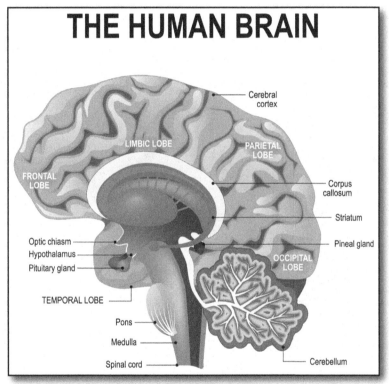

Figure 2.3 Images for the limbic system located in the center of the brain beneath the cerebral cortex.

Finally, the *cerebral cortex* (responsible for conscious thought and voluntary actions) is the last to develop. It is the surface of the cerebrum and is made of gray matter that is filled with wrinkles and folds. It's what we see when we look at a picture of the human brain.

This is where all the senses report their findings and make sense of the environment. It is divided into four lobes or parts that work together to produce appropriate responses and control of the body. I believe the cerebral cortex represents the essence of who we are and who we are going to become, mind, body, and spirit/emotions. It is the physical embodiment of the whole child.

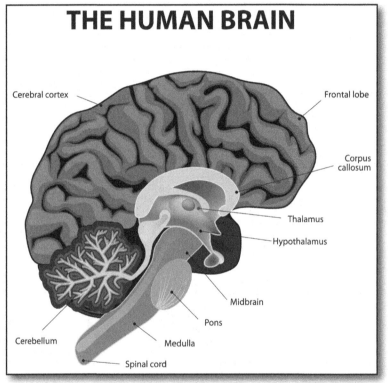

Figure 2.4 Overall view of cerebral cortex, the top layer of the cerebrum, which is referred to as gray matter, and is the last part of brain to develop. It is responsible for conscious thought and voluntary actions.

Individual parts of the cerebrum: frontal lobes, parietal lobes, occipital lobes, and temporal lobes

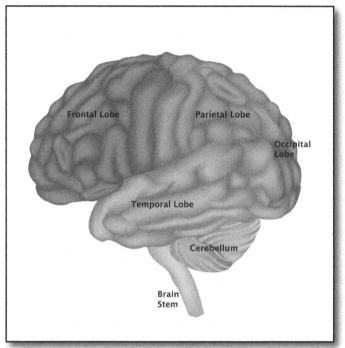

Figure 2.5 The cerebrum is divided into four lobes: the frontal, parietal, occipital, and temporal. 538947429

When you examine this sequence of development and what each area controls, you begin to understand the hierarchy of development and the importance of each area. The limbic system, right in the middle of it all, and the one area that does not control measurable outcomes, in my opinion is probably the most significant in terms of quality of life and social interaction. It is the center of emotional response and memory and along with the senses is the glue that holds us together. The senses will be investigated in the next chapter.

CHAPTER 3

Senses: The Glue that Holds Us All Together

*A*RE YOU GETTING ANY INTERESTING TIDBITS from all this information? I am trying to make this pleasant, informative reading without too much scientific jargon, which would probably bore you. Maybe you're already bored because you've heard all this before, and if that's the case, I apologize. Just keep reading; you might learn something new. However, before we move on, I would like to summarize what the seven senses are and how their functions are essential to positive growth and connectedness in the whole child, physically, mentally, and emotionally.

The seven senses—yes, that's right. I was taught that there were only five, but now science has informed us that there are at *least* seven, with more having recently been identified. For now, I am going to address the seven senses that impact learning the most. Your baby learns from you and connects to you through each of his senses.

- Vestibular (Balance): The movement and balance structures are located in the inner ear. It is *mostly recognized for balance.*
- Proprioceptive System: This system provides for body awareness and position in space. The cells are located in the skin, muscles, ligaments, and joints.

- Tactile (Touch): This sense tells you what is in contact with your body and gives your body information about pain, pressure, temperature, size, texture, and shape.
- Auditory (Hearing): This sense allows you to locate, capture, and discriminate sounds. The receptors are located in the inner ear.
- Gustatory Sense (Taste): This sense gives you information about the things that enter your mouth. It is considered a chemical sense.
- Olfactory (Smell): This sense senses chemicals in the air and gives information about things you smell.
- Visual System (Sight): This sense provides information about color, shape, size, and distance of objects from one another, as well as movement of objects and depth perception.

Scientists have discovered that touch is the first sense to develop in the fetus, at about eight weeks gestational age, which is calculated by the number of weeks from the first day of the last menstrual cycle (BabyCenter, 2015). They have observed how the tiny fetus responds to a mere hair stroke on the cheek. Remember now, I am talking about the baby inside of you. By the time that fetus is thirty-two weeks old, almost every part of the body is sensitive to just a hair stroke. If it's this sensitive to a hair stroke, imagine how sensitive it is to heat, cold, pressure, and pain. Keep this in mind: touch is the very basis of human experience and communication. Remember this fact after your baby is born; touch is so important. What role does touch play in our classrooms today? It's almost forbidden.

How do scientists know a fetus is sensitive to certain stimuli? Advances in technology enable them to see how the fetus responds with movement. While movement or motion is not a so-called sense, it develops along with the senses. With the first heartbeat that occurs three weeks after conception, we see the movement that is the symbol of life itself. The movement of the tiny valves of the heart display movement with life's rhythm.

With that first stroke of hair on the cheek, the fetus moves. Between weeks six and ten, movement becomes a form of exercise. The fetus shows off all of its impressive moves, stretching, turning and rotating the arms, legs, and head, and putting the hand to the face, the hand to mouth, the hand to the head, and one hand to the other hand; all are common occurrences. Opening and closing of the mouth and swallowing are all observable at ten weeks. By fourteen weeks, a complete set of movements has developed. Breathing and jaw movements have begun. By this stage of development, movement can be spontaneous or evoked by something that the mother does or something that occurs around her. For example, between ten and fifteen weeks (gestational age), the fetus moves immediately after the mother sneezes, coughs, or even laughs (The Fetal Senses: A Classical View, 2015). *All this movement in the uterus lets us know that movement is part of learning and the essence of life. What role does movement play in our classrooms?*

This amazing development of motion and movement goes hand in hand with the development of the proprioceptive and vestibular systems. Are you asking yourself, "What the heck are the vestibular and proprioceptive senses?" Well, the vestibular system is constructed of the semicircular canals of the inner ear that registers body movement, the pull of gravity, speeding up and slowing down, sensory integration, and balance. It's the first system to have a response to sensory input and a close relationship to safety and survival (Greutman, 2015). The stimulation of this system is crucial to the child's future ability to partake in everyday physical and academic experiences. Proprioception, in simplified terms, is the body's sense of position in space, motion, and direction regulated by sensory signals sent from the body to the brain. People who move, exercise, and experience different activities have the best-developed vestibular and proprioceptive systems (Baby Presence, 2012). Children need to move. The blueprint is there; we just need to follow it

Between eleven and fifteen weeks, the fetus is opening and closing his mouth and swallowing; it becomes evident that not only the sense of taste has developed, but the sense of smell has also developed. Tests show that swallowing increases with sweet tastes and decreases with bitter and sour tastes. The fetus not only swallows the liquid found in the womb, but it also breathes it. Products of the mother's diet reach the baby through the placenta as well as the blood flowing through the capillaries of the nose. These experiences with tastes and odors can actually have an effect on the baby's breathing and heart rate. For example, in an experiment with mothers drinking coffee, whether caffeinated or decaffeinated, a change in the fetal breathing and heart rate was noted (The Fetal Senses: A Classical View, 2015). *This kind of information should tell the mother to watch what she eats and drinks.*

As teachers, this blueprint of development should inform us that activities that involve food are definitely more memorable than those that do not. Hard to remember spelling words are more likely to be remembered if the words are spelled out with icing that can be tasted or raisins that can be eaten. Just refrain from using nuts, and I'm sure you understand why; so many children are allergic to them. Combine skill acquisition with as many senses as possible to improve memory and retention whenever possible, and while movement is not widely considered a sense, please include it as often as possible. The key to success is to make learning fun, and I repeat, involve as many senses as possible. This encourages the child to be more focused, and it integrates the cognitive with the sensory, which involves more of the whole child. It is compatible with how the brain learns.

Even though the fetus is protected by amniotic fluid, embryonic membranes, the walls of the uterus, and the mother's abdomen, it is still impacted by outside sounds, vibrations, and motions. This brings us to the discussion of the senses of listening and hearing. Studies confirm that the mother's voice is powerful because it reaches the fetus through her own body as opposed to outside sounds. The pattern, pitch, stress, and rhythm of the mother's voice, as well as music, reach the fetus with little distortion. Some sounds actually affect metabolic rate and brain waves. Lullabies and melodic sounds have a positive effect on the fetus. A few seconds of sound can produce an effect on fetal heart rate and movement that lasts up to one hour (Busnel, Granier-Deferre, & Lecanuet, 1992).

FMRIs (Functional Magnetic Resonance Imaging) show changes in a functioning brain and inform us that different kinds of music affect different parts of the brain (Jensen, 2000). Does music play any role in the regular classroom? It did for me; I made it a point to play Beethoven or upbeat music before the math period in spite of the strange looks I received. I learned that math facts are more likely to make it to long-term memory if introduced with rhythm and music. This didn't go over so well with other teachers, but it didn't matter because I knew something they didn't know. This inclusion of music stimulated my students' brains and improved their attitudes toward math. Things that make a difference to the unborn baby in the womb continue to make a difference to the child after birth, in the home, and in the school. The blueprint is there; we just need to use it for construction.

Different sounds have different impacts on the fetus. Although not conclusive, studies suggest that continuous, repeated exposure to extremely loud music, strong vibrations, and industrial noises can im-pact the fetus negatively in different ways. Researchers in Belfast have actually discovered through ultrasound that active listening actually begins before the development of the ear is complete (Loud Noises

During Pregnancy, 2015). So before your pregnancy is obvious, your baby is being affected by the outside world. Once you know you are pregnant, start the sweet sounds like talking and singing to your baby and playing music for it. It might not serve a purpose right now, but who knows? It doesn't hurt to practice. After all, listening occurs before the baby has ears. Who knew?

Are you asking yourself, "How the heck can that happen?" Well, scientists believe it can happen because the very first receptive hearing begins with the skin and the skeleton. These findings indicate how complex hearing is. The skin receives input from touch, vibrations, heat and cold, and pain. This early listening system then receives input from the vestibular system, the inner ear. With this kind of responsive listening and reception system being proven to exist at sixteen weeks, hearing is recognized as a major channel of information gathering that exists about twenty-four weeks before birth. Now that I think about it, I can support the finding about the bones being receptors too. Since I have been a senior citizen, my bones wake me up, telling me that bad weather, usually rain, is in the forecast.

The senses of smell and taste are at a level of complete development at birth, while hearing fully matures at about one month after birth, vision throughout the first year, and the vestibular system continues to develop for the first six years of life. Smell is one of the first senses to develop and is the predominant sense early on in fetal development because smells can pass through the amniotic fluid, which surrounds the fetus. The baby can actually smell the food the mother is eating. A few days after birth, the baby can distinguish between the smell of his mother's breast milk and milk from a different mother.

All of these sensory systems are developing during the same span of time in the fetus and are integrated and depend on each other. Difficulties in one system will most likely impact another system. For example, if your child has problems with balance, there could be a problem with the *visual input system*, for we know that organizing the body for movement is the chief function of the visual system; vision and movement go hand in hand. Vision and smell and vision and taste all work together. When you have a bad cold with a stopped-up nose, you can't taste your food. I hate when that happens, especially if I'm eating sweets.

While we've taken a quick look at some of the sensory organs of the developing fetus, we have to give special attention to the most investigated, celebrated sense, which deserves an in-depth review. Can you guess which sense that would be? Yes, you guessed it—vision.

Vision, considered the most dominant sense after birth, is not feasible to study in the fetus. What we do know now from the ultrasound is that the unborn fetus is very sensitive to light. The heart rate of the fetus increases when a light is shone on the mother's abdomen. Even more fascinating is the fact that while the eyelids of the fetus are fused shut, there seems to be some form of vision in operation that guides them to shrink away from needles entering the womb or even attack the needle with a fist (Birnholz, Stephens, and Faria, 1978).

I can surely support these findings because I have a vivid memory of watching my grandson's 3D ultrasound and how he put his hands over his eyes when the light was projected on his little body. I was amazed, horrified, and saddened by this experience. I realized that advances in science are informative and crucial to growth in knowledge and the well-being of the human race, but at the same time, I wondered if maybe, at times, science isn't going too far. I am not suggesting that we remain stuck in our old ways and not be enlightened by new findings, but some of those old ways developed some pretty fine individuals. Just saying.

CHAPTER 4

Vision, the Amazing Sense

*A*LL THE SENSES ARE AMAZING BY VIRTUE OF what they do, but the most amazing of all is vision, at least that's my opinion, and I am in very good company when I say this. Vision is the process used to make sense of the environment. Research reports that an estimated 80 to 85 percent of our cognition, perception, and learning in general is processed through the visual system. Consequently, it is viewed as the dominant sense.

While this sense is so extraordinary, remember that it is one of the senses that finishes its development after birth and one of the senses that you can consciously impact. Vision and how the brain uses visual information is a learned skill. This means there are many chances for error along the developmental path. That's huge! You can truly make a difference in the development of this sense by what you do and how you do it.

Since the way the brain uses visual information is a learned skill, it's important that you think about your baby's environment throughout each day. The effect that light has on the unborn child should give us clues about how light affects the child after birth. Too much sunlight can be harmful to the skin, and direct sunlight can damage the eyes. What about the benefits of natural sunlight? Children need to spend more time outside in natural light to help with the need for Vitamin D. Instead of spending more time in natural daylight, they are constantly being exposed to the artificial blue end of the light spectrum emitted by TVs, computers, and other digital devices. The Vision Council reports that one in four children use one or more of these devices more than three hours a day, usually more, because the usage occurs at school and at home, in addition to the time spent on them between school and home (The Vision Council, 2015). Researchers for the US Centers for Disease Control and Prevention found that almost 75 percent of children between the ages of twelve and fifteen years of age spent at least two hours a day watching TV and using computers; this time did not include phones or other digital devices. Extended exposure to digital devices can lead to vision issues (AOA, 2016).

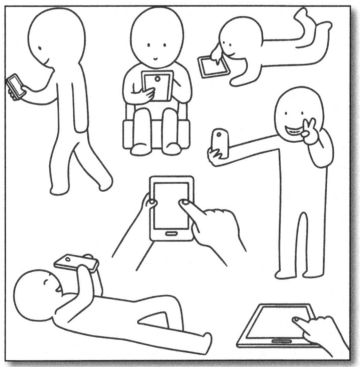

Figure 4.1 Children's brains ruled by handheld devices.

It's common knowledge that UV rays emitted by the sun can be harmful to the eyes, but artificial blue light emissions over time can be even more harmful to the eyes. I realize how difficult it is to monitor your child's time spent on these various devices, but do the very best you can with leveraging allowances, giving rewards, or whatever it takes to protect your child's vision.

Light, in spite of some of its negative attributes, does play a very essential role in the development of vision. As the parent of a newborn, one of the first things you can do is alternate sides when nursing or giving your baby a bottle every day, throughout the day, so that light hits the baby's eyes from different positions. You should also make sure that your baby spends time outside, taking rides in the stroller, or just sitting on the patio where he or she can use his or her eyes to focus on things in the distance. This is very important for optimal eye development.

If you are communicating with your baby, you should be noticing what his eyes are doing. Between birth and six weeks of age, your baby should be staring at surroundings, blinking when a camera flashes, and holding his or her gaze on bright lights or objects. Since muscles and focus are not mature yet, the baby's eyes may be misaligned or turn in at times. The eyes and head usually turn together during this stage of eye development. Between eight and twenty-four weeks, the eyes begin to follow moving objects and people, and they can do this without much head movement. Your baby is becoming an investigator; he or she is examining his or her hands, food, bottle, and everything in his or her surroundings. The older your baby gets, the more interested he or she becomes in his or her environment. Your baby will look around the room to see what is happening and will look for dropped toys. All this activity is great, but the most exciting thing that your baby is likely to do between thirty to forty-eight weeks is visually respond to your face and voice. By the time your child is one year to a year and a half old, he or she is interested in pictures, points to objects in the distance, and holds objects in his or her hands very close as he or she inspects them. Don't be alarmed if your baby's eyes turn in while examining objects close to his or her face; that's perfectly normal. By the time your child turns two and a half, you can do more exercises or activities with him or her to make developmental progress easier and more beneficial.

There are little tests that you can do at home to check your child's vision development (BabyCenter, 2015). For example:

-Hold your child's favorite toy, (or maybe you should just choose an interesting toy so that he or she doesn't snatch it out of your hand), eight to ten inches away from his or her face and ask him or her to follow the toy with just his or her eyes.

-Tell your child to keep his or her head still and use only his or her eyes. Move the toy back and forth and up and down at a moderate speed. Check to make sure that the child's eyes are in alignment with the toy while it is moving.

-Next, point out an object across the room. Using the same toy, tell your child to look from the toy to the object without moving his or her head. He or she should be able to do this without much head movement. Model these exercises for your child if he or she has problems, but be sure to make a mental note as to whether he or she can do these exercises successfully.

Another quick test can be used to see if your child is using both eyes to look at the same object, to see if they are working together and blending both fields of view.

- Hold a playing card over one of your child's eyes and tell him or her to look at that same toy that you should hold about six inches from his or her nose. Once your child has focused on the toy, quickly remove the card. Up to the age of three, the uncovered eye will take a minute to adjust while it finds the toy. By four or four and a half, the adjustment should be very slight.

Once you have determined that your child is using both eyes and blending both fields of vision, you need to find out if both eyes are seeing with equal clarity. One eye could be seeing a blurry picture while the other eye sees an object clearly. It's very difficult to see details if both eyes aren't seeing the same clear picture.

Check for clarity of vision in both eyes.

- Use the playing card to cover one eye, and ask your child to describe objects at a distance in detail. Tell him or he to mention everything he or she can see that would describe the objects.

- Next, put the card over the other eye and repeat this process. Your child should be able to describe the objects with the same amount of detail, but not being able to do this might indicate the need for professional attention.

Once your child begins school, most of his or her vision skills will be used for reading. Consequently, you should try this exercise with a picture book and ask him or her to describe pictures. Cover one eye and describe the pictures in detail, and then cover the other and do the same thing. Hopefully the level of detail will be the same, or at least very similar. Once again, if you observe a discrepancy between the two eyes, seek the help of a behavioral optometrist.

The tests you can do at home are prerequisites for the skills needed in school and are indicators that can point out potential problems; they cannot take the place of a comprehensive vision exam. Look for a behavioral or developmental optometrist to check your child's vision; it makes a big difference in what the doctor is looking for and how he or she goes about correcting problems.

Children should undergo eye exams before starting school, and preferably these exams should be performed by a behavioral optometrist in addition to a regular optometrist. What most parents and educators don't understand is that eyesight is acuity. It's what the eye sees when light hits an object, but vision is a lot more complicated.

Vision is in the brain, and it is what makes sense of all you see in your environment.

We all say that we see with our eyes, but vision is processed in the brain, the occipital lobe at the back of the brain. The visual cortex is one of the most powerful parts of the brain, with approximately forty different specialized modules. The region of the brain that processes touch is directly connected to the visual cortex. Hearing and touching have a definite effect on visual perception.

Haptics, a fairly new area of study in sensory processing, informs us that the sense of touch, as well as the vision sense, affects the way in which we interpret and interact with the world (Shaymansky, J. & Wesson, K. 2012). Touch helps promote the brain's ability to visualize. As a classroom teacher, I used this knowledge to provide practice for my students. Once a week, on Touch Tuesday, I would provide a bag of objects that the children would investigate by putting their hand in the bag, touching and manipulating the objects with their eyes closed. After one minute, they would make a list of as many objects as possible. The three students with the highest number of correctly identified objects won prizes. The class loved this activity, and they were developing their abilities to visualize while having fun. This activity was a great way to develop a skill set that would definitely enhance their reading comprehension. Being able to interpret and visualize what you are reading is what makes reading enjoyable and worthwhile.

We also did special activities that involved hearing and visualization. I would play different kinds of sounds as well as different types of music and have children draw what they were imagining or visualizing while listening. This activity was so interesting and informative as to the innermost emotions and overall makeup of each child.

Have you ever watched that *Febreze* commercial where what was being smelled provided a visual image? This is what happens all the time. It's so spontaneous that we don't think about it. It even works with taste. If you are blindfolded and told to bite an onion, when in fact it is an apple, you will see yourself biting an onion. Your taste will tell you that you are biting an onion. It's so amazing.

Our vision system is so powerful; it works with every other sense to interpret the environment. It is even working in our dreams. Just think about it; dreams are made of images and scenes that reflect the present environment, emotionally charged situations or memories, and even occurrences within your body. What do I mean by "present environment and occurrences within your body"? Well, this is what I'm talking about.

I vividly remember how exciting it was to realize that your brain makes sense of what your senses are reporting, even while you are sleeping. I remember dreaming that a little Cocker Spaniel was clawing at the kitchen floor while trying to get a toy that was under the table. The sound of his clawing got so loud that it awakened me from my dream, and I woke to find out that my sister was unwrapping candy in my ear to wake me up. My brain created images that matched the sensory input. This is what I was referring to when I mentioned present environment.

Throughout my childhood, until I reached my early twenties, I had a recurring dream in which I was swimming in a pool underwater and trying to get to the top to get air. I always felt the fear of drowning, but at the last minute, I would reach the top and gasp for air. Can you guess what was happening with my body? I found out later that I was suffering from sleep apnea. I suppose I grew out of it because I haven't had that dream for years. I've had many other dreams that provided evidence of how the senses were connected in doing the job that God planned for them to do, but I won't bore you with them. You can probably think of your own.

I shared these memories with you to emphasize the enormous role that vision plays in our daily lives. If you can effect positive change in your child's vision, doesn't it make sense to do so?

Your child can visit the office of an optometrist and take tests that would determine that your child has 20/20 vision, and this would be accurate if you are only looking at acuity, but there's so much more to vision that needs to be addressed. Thousands of children begin school with 20/20 acuity but suffer from vision dysfunction, which is never discovered. Glasses are prescribed to fix any existing problems, while vision therapy is what's needed.

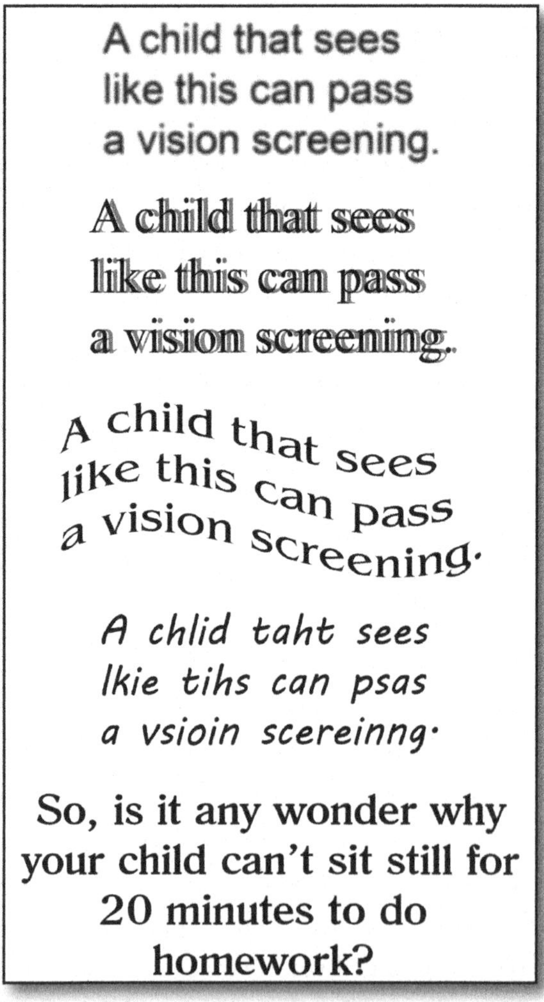

A child that sees like this can pass a vision screening.

A child that sees like this can pass a vision screening.

A child that sees like this can pass a vision screening.

A chlid taht sees lkie tihs can psas a vsioin scereinng.

So, is it any wonder why your child can't sit still for 20 minutes to do homework?

Figure 4.2 Simple vision screening is not enough.

By the way, vision therapy centers around the country recommend that you have your baby's vision checked by a developmental, behavioral optometrist as early as six months of age.

Chances are, you've never heard of vision dysfunction, but not to fear, it will be covered in part III, "The Third Dimension of Learning."

CHAPTER 5

Science Should Inform Parenting and Education

SO HOW SHOULD ALL THIS SCIENCE IMPACT US? Well, it tells us that once a woman begins thinking about getting pregnant, she should be aware of what she does and what goes on in the environment around her.

The sequence and hierarchy of the way senses develop in the embryo give us clues about their interconnectedness and importance. The sensory systems develop in close association with each other because many facets of the stimulation of the senses have to coordinate with other senses in order for them to function at their best, and this holds true throughout life.

Here's a little clue. Have you ever been listening to the radio while driving, when suddenly a storm hits? I don't know about you, but when that happened to me, the first thing I did was turn down my radio. I have discovered that it is a common reaction because we are trying to cut off the connection to the auditory system so we can give more power to the visual one. If they weren't connected, it wouldn't matter.

The baby's first months in the womb are demonstrative of the fact that nothing develops in isolation and that all sensory modes give us so much information about the integrated design of the senses and the developing individual it is to become. We know how taste and smell work in tandem, how skin and bone contribute to an early hearing system, and how some inexplicable form of vision seems to be working, even though the eyes have not yet opened. When the fetus experiences pain, it reacts with strenuous body movement and vigorous breathing, in addition to increased hormone production. Within ten minutes of needling the fetus's vein for a transfusion, the fetus shows a tremendous rise in hormones that are indicative of pain. Ultrasounds have recorded fetuses sucking their thumbs and getting erections, sometimes simultaneously, which suggests that self-stimulation for pleasure is already occurring. Experiments have shown that the fetus reacts strongly to even very low amounts of alcohol introduced to the mother's system. Breathing stops, and this break in breathing can last for over thirty minutes. As mentioned earlier, fetuses have been observed to shrink away from a needle entering their space as well as attacking it if they are nicked. After an experience like this, the heart rate of some fetuses hit new highs, and their breathing motions do not return to normal for a few days. Researchers have discovered that babies are dreaming as early as twenty-three weeks gestational age (time lapsed from first day of the last menstrual period to the present time). These dreams are indicated by REM (rapid eye movement), just as in adults, and often include body movement and pleasant or unpleasant facial expressions (Chamberlain, 2013). These expressions stem from mental and emotional experiences within the fetus. Yes, that's right; your baby experiences emotions in the uterus, and the way you handle emotions and deal with stress while pregnant has an effect on your baby. It continues to have an effect after your baby is born.

Throughout the first dimension of learning and development, the fetus has learned what tastes it prefers, what odors are pleasant, how its mother's voice sounds, what kind of music it likes to hear, how to move in different situations, and so many other things that prepare it for the second dimension of learning: life outside the womb. Hopefully, with the knowledge of how all the body systems work together, how toward the end of the trimester even the mental and emotional abilities of the fetus are coming into play, you are getting the whole picture; the connectedness of the whole child and how the different learning environments play such a crucial role in the child's wellbeing.

What we see emerging is the fact that movement and emotions go hand in hand with learning and development. We see how the senses are interpreting the environment and making sense of it. The foundation of learning and the hard wiring of the brain-body connection are evident, even in the womb.

As a parent, it should make you more aware that your baby is a real human being with emotions and needs that have to be met for survival. As educators, it should cause us to consider the importance and relevance of music, movement, and sensory-packed experiences in the classroom. As a politician, it should make you reconsider the present state of teaching mandates prescribed by state educational guidelines that are on the verge of removing physical education, art, music, and worst of all kindergarten play time. You may be wondering what is so important about kindergarten play time. Well, I will explain in part III, "The Third Dimension of Learning."

PART II

The Second Dimension of Learning and Development: Learning in the Home, Where Parenting Makes the Difference

CHAPTER 6

Emotions and Sensory Experiences

*A*T FIRST BABIES DON'T KNOW THAT YOU ARE there to feed and comfort them, but they find out by expressing their needs, whether they be physical or emotional, through crying. They are learning *Communications 101*, and it is your job as the parent to respond, by making the baby feel safe and comfortable. Babies are like sponges, absorbing everything in their environment. Whatever they hear, smell, taste, touch, or see sends information to the limbic system, the center of emotions, and then to the cerebral cortex, where they make meaning out of all this information. All the information your baby takes in is connected to emotions. Whether they are good or bad is up to you. Look in your baby's face as you talk to him or her. He or she doesn't mind if you don't have on any makeup. Establish eye contact and know that your baby is remembering your face, your voice, and your smell, hopefully a good one. Do not smoke and get in your baby's face. Allan Greene, MD, professor of pediatrics at Stanford University, and author of *Raising Baby Greene,* reports that scientific experiments show that even in the womb, babies cringe when exposed to cigarette smoke. Try to be mindful of unpleasant body odor when you're in your baby's face. He might grow to love this smell, and that wouldn't be such a good thing. I'm just saying.

On the other side of that coin, babies do like pleasant, soothing smells like lavender. They are also comforted by clothing that has been worn by their mothers. I can remember my mother putting my robe in the crib with my daughter to help her go to sleep. I didn't totally understand the significance of that because that was before research and the discovery of how emotions are connected to the senses. Grandmothers instinctively know what to do; at least mine could have informed science.

The average first-time parent feels overwhelmed during the newborn's first month of life. It is normal to be confused as well as frustrated by all the things you have been told to do and look out for; this is totally understandable. Remember to take a deep breath, exhale, and keep your baby fed, dry, and safe, but that's only part of it; the most important way to help your baby grow and develop in an emotionally healthy environment is to communicate with him. At all times, restrain yourself; do not yell or show anger toward your baby. He's only doing what he was born to do. Assure your baby that you are there to love and care for him; be reminded that this new environment is quite different from the one he just left. Just think about it. How well could you adjust to living underwater?

Research shows that the unborn infant responds to the mother's use of a high-pitched voice, and that response continues after birth (Babycentre, 2016). Gently hug, touch, and kiss your baby. This provides rich stimulation, comfort, and loving attention that enhances your baby's emotional well-being and stability and prepares him for future life in society. Everything you do serves a purpose, hopefully the right one. For example, talking to your baby while changing diapers and during bathing support language acquisition skills, but here's a tip about an exception to this; stop talking while you're breastfeeding, because babies like peace and quiet while nursing. Enhance every activity you do with your baby by integrating it with loving forms of physical and verbal communication. Spend as much time as possible carrying your baby against your chest so he can feel your heartbeat and body rhythms. Tickle and massage your baby's feet; there are lots of sensory receptors in the human foot. Loving emotions and movement connected to daily activities provide for a healthy development.

Figure 6.1 Sensory experiences

This mother is doing something that most caregivers do without realizing its importance. This activity is not only an expression of love; it is a sensory experience that actually stimulates the vestibular system.

CHAPTER 7

That Very Special Milestone

*A*S YOUR BABY GROWS, YOU WILL NOTICE HOW much he or she changes from day to day, week to week month to month. What you are noticing are developmental stages and milestones of your child's development. Some of these changes will be minor, but many of them will be accompanied by a big band, applause, and much fanfare. I think you could name a few of those times—for example, when your baby says, "Ma Ma" (most seem to say "Da Da" first), or pulls up to a standing position.

There is no need to dig deeply into most milestones because they are self-explanatory and you will recognize them when you experience them. However, there is one milestone in particular that warrants some discussion—crawling. Please do not rush your baby through this stage by encouraging him to walk or by forcing him to stand on wobbly legs not ready to hold his weight. Provide "belly time," which strengthens the neck and back muscles and upper body strength for your baby. Time spent on the belly naturally leads to creeping and/or some type of mobility for most babies.

While babies crawl in different ways, asymmetry in crawling (using one side only for attempting to crawl) can be a sign of a problem. It might not mean anything in the case of your child, but just for peace of mind, have your baby see a pediatric physical therapist.

Most babies will crawl when they are ready, but there are ways to encourage your baby to crawl (BabyCentre, 2016).

- Give your baby plenty of tummy time, and avoid leaving baby in walkers or bouncers for long periods of time throughout the day.
- While your baby is on the floor on his tummy, place toys just out of reach around him.
- Get down on the floor with your baby and model desired behaviors.

There are some babies who don't crawl and they are fine, but you should encourage crawling because there are several benefits to crawling. Crawling helps reduce the primitive reflexes in the brain, so that advanced, normal movement and neurological organization can develop (The Learning Clinic, 2016). Say what? Do you know what primitive reflexes are? Well, while babies are in the uterus, primitive reflex movements help develop the baby's brain. They are actually the basis of our nervous system and our ability to move. These movements are responsible for the neural or nerve connections between different areas of the brain. They are repetitive, automatic movements that are necessary for the development of head control, muscle tone, the vestibular system, and sensory integration; they are the foundation of our lifelong reflexes. If these reflexes remain in the brain stem where they originate, without making connections to the prefrontal cortex, the area of the brain where information is analyzed and processed, then we would always be in survival mode and unable to think and make intelligent decisions about stressful situations. These connections are important later on for learning, behavior, communication, and emotional well-being (Blog Epic Health Services, 2015).

Primitive or newborn reflexes remain present at birth in a normally developing infant; it's how they respond automatically to certain stimuli. Each primitive reflex is associated with one or more of the sensory processing systems and can affect auditory, taste, tactile, smell, visual, vestibular, and proprioception. For example, the ATNR or asymmetrical tonic neck reflex is something you might have seen but did not think of as an automatic repeatable response to something. You can observe the ATNR occurring when a baby turns its head to one side and the limbs on that side straighten, while the limbs on the other side flex or bend. ATNR should disappear by the time the baby is six months old. The important thing to note is that if ATNR is retained, it can cause problems with the child's learning process. It can interfere with handwriting. When the child has to turn his head to look at the board or page, his arm wants to extend and his fingers want to open. It's the same thing that happens to infants, only they don't have to worry about writing anything. Consequently, attempting to hold a pen or pencil for a long time will require lots of effort. To compensate for this, the child grips the pencil very tightly, which results in body tension. With so much energy being used to hold onto the pencil, little to no energy is left for concentrating on the content of the assignment. Children who are affected by this primitive reflex demonstrate a fear of writing or anxiety when asked to write. If asked to respond to a question in writing, the child may appear to be negative and unresponsive, yet if he were asked to respond to the same question orally, he could do so with no problem.

ATNR can also interfere with reading, eye tracking in particular. If the eyes do not move smoothly from one side of the page to another, the child can lose his place, which can lead to a loss of comprehension. When you think about it, the smallest things can result in the child losing attention. ATNR is also thought to be the cause of several other fairly common conditions.

While there are about seventy identified primary reflexes, I am only interested in the ones that are known to impact education and academic skills. When these primary reflexes are retained, they can interfere with the development of natural, automatic skills and control (Blomberg, 2015). In summary, symptoms include the following:

- Dyslexia
- Poor coordination
- Sensory integration disorder (sensory processing disorder)
- Disorganization
- Language and speech delays
- Fidgeting
- Poor concentration
- Poor bladder control
- Problem skin
- Muscle tone
- Muscle weakness
- Breathing problems
- Asthma
- Low endurance
- Fatigue
- Chronic body aches and pains

STNR or symmetric tonic neck reflex is more a transitional reflex than a primitive one. It allows the baby to bend its legs and straighten its arms when it looks up, so movement of the head is linked to movement of the arms and legs. It helps the baby transition from lying on its back to crawling, but if retained, can also interfere with the learning process. As the child matures, these reflexes should disappear for the most part and evolve into more complex movement patterns. If primitive reflexes like symmetric tonic neck reflex and asymmetric tonic neck reflex don't disappear after nine months, several problems will become evident that can negatively affect the child's academic success.

The Moro reflex is another primitive reflex that warrants discussion. If retained, it can also produce negative effects on academic progress The Moro reflex occurs when the baby feels as though it's falling and should disappear by about five months of age. This reflex is replaced by the startle reflex. This reflex is the response to unexpected change, like loud noises, sudden movement, or a sensation of falling or lack of support. Retention of this reflex results in poor coordination, sensitivity to bright lights, allergies, lower immunity, mood swings, frequent ear and throat infections, lack of learning from experience, poor stamina, the need to be in control, and many other conditions.

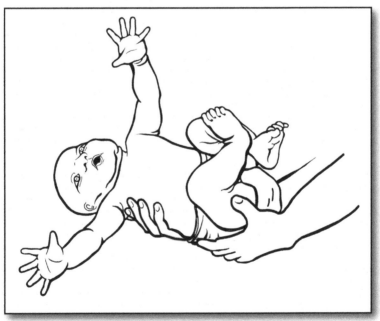

Figure 7.1 (Moro Reflex, Illustrated by Brenda Hunter, 2017)

Research has shown that children who have disabilities usually have retained one or more primitive reflexes. If ATNR and STNR, along with many of the other reflexes, remain in use, and are not integrated into the nervous system, they can make the life of the child and his or her teacher a nightmare. The impact that they can have on a child can cause him or her to have a lifetime of lacking confidence, addiction, and a feeling of overwhelm. Thank God that many children have the ability to compensate for some of the shortcomings they experience from retained primitive reflexes.

ATNR, STNR, and the Moro reflex are just three of the seventy identified primitive reflexes. Many of these reflexes have overlapping consequences, and a few of them actually remain with us throughout our adult lives. A few additional primitive reflexes that can be easily checked and observed in the home or school are listed at the end of this chapter. Answering the questions and having your child do the exercises can provide crucial information as to whether your child may have retained some primitive reflexes.

Please make sure that your baby gets plenty of tummy time (floor time), so that he or she can experiment with large muscle movement and stretch his or her limbs. Your baby won't be able to do this if he or she is put in a swing or infant seat for hours each day. Placing your child in a walker or a playpen is more acceptable and beneficial to his or her development than leaving him or her in a swing. I am not saying that you should not put your baby in a swing, for it can be calming and emotionally soothing, but I am saying that you shouldn't use the swing as a babysitter by leaving your baby in it for long periods of time. I get emotional about this because I've seen it happen a lot.

On a more positive note, crawling helps babies integrate their primitive reflexes into more advanced movements. Crawling helps develop the concept of distance and depth perception. They learn how to navigate to get to toys or things they want to examine more closely; and they develop upper body strength. The cross-lateral movement stimulates both sides of the brain. When a baby crawls, she has to determine where she wants to go and physically moves in that direction; a sense of focus and purposefulness develops. Her eyes and hands work together to establish the first test of eye-hand coordination. The proper development of this skill is crucial for future endeavors like reading, writing, and sports activities, just to name a few.

In addition to eye-hand coordination, crawling helps develop binocular vision (both eyes work together) and accommodation, which demands that the eyes look out in the distance at an object and then back at the hands while crawling. The skill of accommodation is constantly used in school when the child has to look from a book or paper on his desk and then back to the blackboard or screen.

That's why it's so important that you encourage your baby to crawl, and once she starts, don't try to hurry the process, and don't allow in-laws and relatives to do it either. Too many parents hate the crawling stage and want it to be done with because they can't wait for their child to walk; they want their freedom to read a book, watch TV, or delete e-mails, none of which should be done if your baby is crawling around on the floor. Oh, and some parents want "bragging rights" about their child walking early. If they knew the importance of this stage of development, they would regret having tried to speed it up.

You might be surprised at how seriously some parents, especially fathers, take a child's ability to walk early. I am going to share a news story with you about this very topic. In Cincinnati, March 2016, a young mother was arrested along with her boyfriend for faking a kidnapping and seriously injuring a ten-month-old baby. When the boyfriend was asked why he beat the infant, he responded that he was angry with him for not being able to walk. This was an incredible act of cruelty and ignorance fueled by a belief system that supports and glorifies early everything.

Just like learning and development in the womb, learning and development in the first three years of life is most crucial. It is interconnected, sequential, and predictable. Development occurs in a predictable order, from simple to more complex, and provides milestones that can be used to check your child's progress. Keep in mind that children develop at their own rate, but within a reasonable span of time. There are several websites that are very informative about the child's development, as to what you should see at different ages but what about some of those weird actions that you have tried to ignore? They are not so-called milestones but seem to be actions that interfere with the perfect attainment of milestones. A child who learns to walk but trips or stumbles constantly might give you cause to worry and wonder, "What's going on?" Well, the problem could be that the child has retained some *primitive or neonatal reflexes.*

Giving your child lots of belly time as well as opportunities to explore his environment is crucial to well-rounded development and sensory integration. The lack of these opportunities can lead to sensory processing disorder, retaining neonatal reflexes, and less-than-optimal academic success.

A list of a few additional primitive reflexes, including questions and exercises, has been included to promote awareness.

These questions have been modified from *Attention, Balance and Coordination: the ABCs of learning success* by Sally Goddard Blythe (2009).

Retained Primitive Reflexes—Common Questions that Could Suggest Retention

In the Womb-After Birth

- When you were pregnant, did you have any medical problems?
- Was your child delivered at term or early/late?
- Was the birth process unusual in any way (forceps, suction, C-section, induction)?
- Was your child small for term?
- Were there any unusual physical signs (jaundice, bruising, distorted skull)?
- Was there any difficulty feeding or keeping it down? Did your child easily feed off both breasts?
- Between six to eighteen months, was your child demanding, or quiet and unresponsive?
- Did your child develop a violent rocking motion when standing or sitting?

In the Home

- Was your child a head-banger?
- Did your child start walking before ten months or after sixteen months?
- Did your child skip the cross-crawling stage?
- Was your child late when learning to talk (two to three words by two years)?
- Did your child experience any serious illness or seizures in the first eighteen months of life?
- Was there any sign of eczema, asthma, or allergies?
- Did your child have any adverse reactions to vaccinations?
- Did your child have difficulty learning to dress him/herself?
- Did your child wet the bed regularly past the age of five?

- Does your child suffer from travel/motion sickness?
- Did your child have trouble establishing which hand to use or crossing the middle of his body with objects?

At School

- Did your child have problems learning to read and/or write in the early years of school?
- Did your child have difficulty telling the time on an analogue clock?
- Did your child have difficulty riding a bicycle?
- Did your child suffer from recurrent sinus infections, ear infections, or headaches?
- Did your child have difficulty catching a ball?
- Does your child have a problem sitting still?
- Does your child make numerous mistakes when copying from the board?
- Does your child occasionally miss letters or write them backward?
- Does your child have an awkward pencil grip?
- Has your child ever been diagnosed with any conditions such as low muscle tone or ADHD?
- If there is sudden noise, would your child overreact?

If you have answered yes to a majority of these questions, then it is likely that further investigation from an RNR (retained natal reflexes) practitioner would most likely reveal an immature central nervous system, indicating the retention of some primitive reflexes.

Home Tests

Here is a collection of tests for you to do at home with your children. They are designed to indicate the likelihood of retained neonatal reflexes (Sally Goddard Blyth, 2009).

If it's certain that these reflexes have been retained, then the child may be trying to give you warning signs in her everyday activities; these symptoms are listed under each of the specific reflexes.

Look with eyes that see. Keep your eyes open to see additional signs of difficulty, and with this understanding you can repeat these tasks at home. This can also serve to help the child realize the difficulty involved while performing a seemingly simple task. It can open your eyes to see that the child is not failing to perform due to lack of trying but due to a lack of communication between brain and body, something beyond his control.

Certain tests can help to discover if the child has retained the impulsive muscle pattern of the reflexes.

Testing for the Asymmetric Tonic Neck Reflex (ATNR)

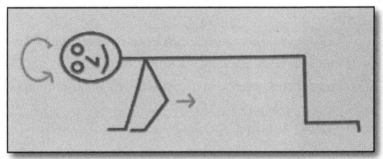

Figure 7.3 Test for Primitive Reflex (Illustrated by Matt Brady, 2009)

A. Ask the child to get on all fours with the arms straight, fingers pointing forward and the head in neutral. With their weight over their hands, the parent rotates the child's head left or right. If their elbow bends on the opposite side of head rotation (as would in the infant) or the weight shifts to the back and legs, (i.e., off the hands), then the reflex is probably present.

B. Alternately, have the child stand with arms straight out in front of her at shoulder height. Ask the child to turn her head fully to the left or fully to the right while maintaining the position of the arms out front. If the torso and arms turn in the direction of the head or if the arms drop, this reflex is likely present. This signifies that the child has not yet disassociated neck movement from shoulder movement.

Testing for the Sagittal Tonic Labyrinthine Reflex

A. Lying facedown on the ground with palms facing down, ask the child to hold the head off the ground and raise the legs, simultaneously keeping the legs straight (a.k.a., the Superman). If he is unable to keep his legs straight then the sagittal TLR is probably present.

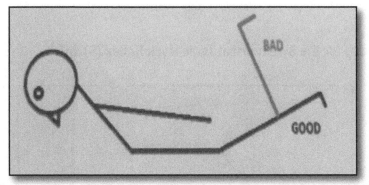

Figure 7.4 Tests for Primitive Reflex (Illustrated by Matt Brady, 2009)

B. This one is great performed with music. Place a like-colored sticker on the right hand and left knee and a different like-colored sticker on the left hand and right knee. Ask the child to march on the spot as she taps her hand to her opposite knee as to match up the stickers. If she turns on the spot, her rhythm is off, or if she begins to tap the same-sided leg, this reflex is likely to be retained. This is a great way to detect gross motor control issues, and if the child displays more difficulty when moving to the beat of the music, it may signify auditory processing issues.

Testing for the Galant Reflex

With the child on all fours, lightly stroke down one side of the lumbar spine toward the sacrum. If he moves his back (typically arching or away from the stroke) then the reflex is probably present.

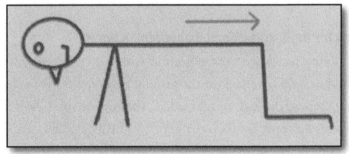

Figure 7.5 Tests for Primitive Reflex (Illustrated by Matt Brady, 2009)

Testing for the Symmetrical Tonic Neck Reflex (STNR)

Figure 7.6 Tests for Primitive Reflex (Illustrated by Matt Brady, 2009)

With the child on all fours with the weight forward over her hands, the parent flexes the neck fully (looking down) and holds for five seconds, then slowly extends the neck (looking up) and holds for five seconds. Repeat three times. If the child alters her body position in any way then the reflex is probably present.

Look for:

- shifting of weight backward
- arching back
- bending arms

During all these tests, it is okay to ask the child to try and hold the requested posture.

Testing for Isolated Upper and Lower Body Movements

By age eight to ten years, a child should be able to isolate his leg rotation from that of his upper body. This isolation of muscle control relies on postural reflexes and appropriate tone in the body's extensors (i.e., the muscles that keep him upright, mostly placed on the backside of his body).

A. Ask the child to walk forward and backward with her feet turned outward (a.k.a., duck walk). If you notice any of the following, then there is a high chance your child has retained the Moro reflex.

Figure 7.7 Test for Primitive Reflex (Illustrated by Matt Brady, 2009)

- can't turn her feet outward
- bending forward
- arms/hands turning outward
- an inability to walk smoothly

B. Ask your child to walk forward and backward with his toes pointing in (a.k.a., pigeon toed). If you notice any of the following, there is high chance your child has retained the Moro reflex.

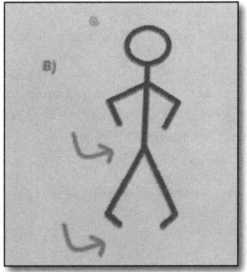

Figure 7.8 Test for Primitive Reflex (Illustrated by Matt Brady, 2009)

- can't turn her feet inward
- bending forward
- arms/hands turning inward
- an inability to walk smoothly

Of course, if you have any suspicions that your child may still be displaying these reflexes, whether by answering yes to some or all of the above questions, by noticing some of the symptoms outlined in each of the reflexes, or by performing some of these at home tests, find a practitioner to help treat your child. Occupational therapy would be a good place to start.

The retention of primitive reflexes can be caused by various factors. A traumatic birth experience or C-section, falls, lack of tummy time, delayed or skipped crawling, chronic ear infections, and head trauma can result in retained primitive reflexes.

These retained primitive reflexes can also lead to autism, ADHD, sensory processing disorder, and learning disabilities (Melillo, R. 2016). When a child is not able to replace primitive reflexes with a more mature system, he will experience difficulty in processing sensory information. Dr. Melillo says that experience and years of research teach us that the best way to inhibit these retained reflexes is to use them. If your child is diagnosed with one or more retained primitive Reflexes, you can get a head start on the therapy by doing some exercises at home.

These exercises are aimed at the five retained reflexes that are usually connected to a brain imbalance.

1. **Face Stroking for Root and Suck Reflex**: Lightly stroke with a small brush or finger from the outer corners of the nose to the corners of the mouth. Repeat five or six times in a row.

2. **Starfish for the Moro Reflex**: Have child sit in fetal position with wrists and ankles crossed right over left. Ball up fists, and take in a deep breath. Next, tell child to fling out arms, stretch out legs, open and stretch out hands, and hold back head to look like a starfish. Have him hold this position while holding his breath for about seven seconds. Finally, have child exhale and repeat by going back to the original position.

3. **Snow Angels for Galant Reflex**: Have child lie face-up on floor with legs straight and arms at the sides. Have her take in a deep breath while spreading legs outward and raising arms overhead to make hands touch. The hands should touch at the same time the legs are fully opened. Repeat.

4. **Ball Squeezes and Finger Wiggling for Palmer Grasp Reflex**: Have child squeeze a small ball like a tennis ball several times in a row. In addition to this exercise, have child stretch arms out in front of him. Tell him to move all ten fingers as though he were playing a piano. Look for wrist flapping, which indicates that small muscles in the hand are not being used. Also, look for mouth and tongue movement. Repeat throughout day.

5. **Fencer Exercise for Asymmetric Tonic Neck Reflex**: Have child sit in a chair and turn head to the right or left. As child turns head, have her stretch out her foot and arm on the same side to which the head is turned and look at her hand. The hand on the opposite side should open, the arm should flex, and the other leg should bend. Repeat three times in a row. (Takes time to perfect.)

Rehabilitating children with an immature central nervous system (CNS) can require the assistance of many health practitioners. These include but are not limited to behavioral optometrists, occupational therapists, physiotherapists, dieticians, naturopaths, sound therapists, play therapists, pediatricians, and general practitioners.

CHAPTER 8

The Role of Emotions and Social Interaction: Newborn to Age Three

*L*EAVING THE SAFETY OF THE WOMB AND COM-ing into this big, scary world with loud noises, bright lights, cameras, and action can be a daunting experience for your baby. You are that baby's safety net. You have to be there to comfort your baby and let him know that he is not all alone. Expect your baby to cry, and get worried if he doesn't, because that would indicate that something's wrong. Babies are supposed to cry; it's their way of communicating with you.

Your infant's emotions play a crucial role in growth and development in all the domains of learning. Just as the limbic system, an important part of the baby's central nervous system, is monitoring emotions and memories, so is the *enteric nervous system.*

Thanks to the *ground*breaking work of Candice Pert, we know how the chemicals inside our bodies form a network that links the mind to the body. In her book *Molecules of Emotion,* she explains how molecules share messages with body and mind, involving emotions, the immune system, as well as the digestive system. When you really think about the ramifications of this research, you realize that the body is actually the unconscious mind. This system is known to respond to emotions and manifest these emotions by feelings in the throat, esophagus, stomach, and intestine (Pert, C. 1997).

Did you hear what I said? That's right; there is another nervous system where neurons are found in the throat, esophagus, and colon that respond to your emotional state of being. According to developmental biologists, a clump of tissue called the neural crest forms early in the embryo's development. One section turns into the central nervous system, while another piece migrates to become the enteric nervous system. The gut's brain, as it is sometimes called, is reported to play a major role in human happiness and misery. Just like you, your baby has an enteric nervous system. She feels sensations of joy, hurt, sadness, and excitement in her little body, and if it's a negative feeling, she will respond naturally by crying.

Each baby is born with his or her own unique personality and temperament. I'm sure you have heard of some of these descriptors: quiet, sensitive, happy, irritable, and demanding. You also have an identifiable temperament, and it's important for you to recognize how your personality traits influence how you respond to your baby.

The way in which you respond to and interact with your baby has an effect on both nervous systems. Take the time to reflect on your own personality and temperament and don't expect your baby to be like you; he's a unique individual who may or may not be like you. Accept your baby's uniqueness; nurture and support him, just the way he is. At the same time, teach your child to accept who he is, and never try to be someone else. Let him know that any person other than himself has already been taken. Just saying.

While your Infant or newborn is unique, there are areas and stages in development that are common to all children. They are usually divided into four areas or domains: *cognitive, language, physical* (fine and gross motor skills), and *social*. These areas are all connected and represent the essence of the whole child, the mind, body, and social/emotions; what happens in one domain influences development in the others. All the learning that took place in the womb serves as the foundation for the more advanced skills and knowledge of the growing child. All learning is accompanied by emotions and enhanced by movement, and I am speaking from my experience as a classroom teacher. By the way, the message in Eric Jensen's book *Learning with the Body in Mind* and lots of scientific research back me up. There are direct connections between the part of the brain that controls movement and the part that controls thinking and learning.

And what does all this have to do with you and your baby? I heard you thinking. Well, in the first three months listen to your baby; she is telling you something. Babies have different-sounding cries for different things. Feel her emotional state. Provide unconditional love and understanding of what your baby is going through. Find out what she likes, what engages her. Move and sing and dance with her to rhythmic music. If you don't have good rhythm, just fake it; your baby won't know the difference, and you are stimulating her vestibular system. Read nursery rhymes that teach rhyming sound patterns and have their own rhythms. These activities will engage your baby, mind, body, and spirit. Your baby will reward all your hugs, kisses, and emotional investment by smiling at you and actually laughing out loud by three months. She will begin to recognize the faces of siblings and other relatives that are seen on a regular basis and enjoy being played with and talked to. Your baby will want to be picked up. Your baby is becoming a very social creature, so she desires and needs social interaction. Your baby's emotional state should come first. This rule of thumb follows the child into the classroom

Positive social interaction comes with a lot of preparation and devotion on a regular basis. Remember patterns, routines, and organization need to begin before birth and continue until your child leaves the nest. It should be based on love and understanding, and if it is, it will make a lasting, positive impact on your child's life. The quality of your infant's emotional/social learning depends on the interactions and relationship that he has with you, the parent, as well as other caregivers. Positive interactions will teach your child to trust and believe that his needs will be met. On the other hand, negative interactions instill mistrust and the feeling that nobody cares. Providing rhythm, routine, and organization to your child's life makes for stability, a sense of knowing and being in control.

When you think about it, you're only following nature's lead. Everything in nature has a sequence and pattern of development. It has an organized way of doing things, so that we know what to expect, how to plan and prepare—well, most of the time. How different and chaotic would life be if we couldn't depend on nature's organization and sequence of events? It's this same principle that should be guiding you as you rear your child.

Children learn emotional/social skills before they learn cognitive skills. For the first three years of life, concentrate on your child's ability to control her emotions, how to be empathetic and considerate of others, how to use her words when upset, how to use good manners, and how to set goals, to name a few. In my opinion, the most important of these would be learning how to control emotions. This is more difficult for boys because of their genetic makeup and the hormones affecting their brains. Therefore it is really important to spend time with your sons on developing this area of emotional output. It will serve him well the rest of his life and could be more important than his A+ report card.

When I make a statement like this, I am speaking from experience as well as research, and I've had more years of teaching experience than I have of research experience. When I reflect on my fourth-grade classes throughout the years, and about the chemistry of different classrooms, I discovered that the leaders were not necessarily the students with the best grades but the students with fairly good grades, great personalities, and a strong sense of who they were. They maintained a positive attitude and never allowed pessimism or anger to overtake them. They didn't allow their emotions to "highjack" their rational thinking, which is amazing at their age, but it demonstrated how home training made a difference. Statistics from research studies give support to what I was experiencing in the classroom. They report that IQ does not necessarily predict a successful life; it accounts for 20 percent of that success, while 80 percent *depends on other factors like, self-motivation, control of emotions, empathy, and optimism* (Goleman, 1996). Believe me, this doesn't just happen within the person; it is a result of social, environmental interactions along the way. I'm sure that my students' gene pools had something to do with it, but nature plus nurture makes an individual who he is.

What does all this mean to you, the parent? It means that you definitely play a role in the development of your child's emotional state. In order for the limbic system, the center of emotions in the brain, to develop normally, certain experiences have to be in place (Greenough, W.T. & Black, J.E. 1992). This system is "experience-expectant"; it needs emotional, social, and maternal stimulation to function properly, and that's where you and all other caregivers come in to play. If this system doesn't receive input like reading faces and body language, making sense of the spoken word, hearing inflections and intonations of the voice, which indicates others' emotions, in addition to many other emotional nuances, chances are it will atrophy or become dysfunctional. Case studies reveal that if a child is separated from her mother right after birth for up to six months or longer, without any social and emotional stimulation, she will develop profound disturbances in social-emotional functioning.

The case of Ted Kaczynski, known as "the Unabomber," provides an example of the results of maternal separation and the lack of emotional stimulation. Ted lived as a hermit in a small, isolated cabin in Montana and was responsible for making bombs that killed several innocent individuals, including children. When Ted was eight or nine months of age, he became ill and had to be hospitalized in isolation for almost two weeks. He was deprived of any contact with his mother as well as anyone else who could provide love and emotional stimulation. After returning home from the hospital, he rejected all forms of affection and totally retreated into himself. He became mean-spirited and sadistic as well as confused; he could not function normally (Joseph, 2015).

What energies are you pouring into your child? How can you help determine the health of your child's dimensions, her physical, mental, emotional, and spiritual well-being? Your child needs:

- Kinetic energy: physical movement and balance exercises
- Mental energy: talking, reading, listening, singing, visual exploration, choice-making opportunities, use of executive functioning
- Emotional/spiritual energy: creating pleasant memories, demonstration of love, compassion, and empathy

Emotions link spirit to body and body to mind. Emotions provide the essence of who we are, and when they are in turmoil; our spirit and body are out of sync. When the child's emotions are in sync, we see the emergence of resilience, a characteristic that is crucial to well-being and success in life. So, be very vigilant and careful with the things you do and say to your child. Caress your child lovingly. Hold him when he is emotionally distraught; give him a sense of security while telling him that everything is going to be all right in God's perfect timing. He might not understand what you're saying at the moment, but if you continue to make statements like this, he will understand one day. This statement carries a lot of weight, because it's really saying that there are things in this world that are beyond your control, and those are the things that you let God handle. The rest you have to handle in the most positive way you can. Talking to your child in this way plants the seeds of resiliency, a characteristic that is crucial to survival.

Even then, in spite of all that you do, your child could develop characteristics that you would never expect, characteristics that make you wonder about family traits and backgrounds. I've heard friends say that their child acts just like one of their grandparents. How does that happen? How is it that the child can exhibit the nonphysical characteristics of their ancestors, especially the ones that they've never met? Have you ever heard of *epigenetics? If you haven't, allow me to enlighten you. At least I will try.*

Epigenetics is the study of processes that alter gene expression without changing DNA. It literally means, "in addition to changes in genetic sequence" (Weinhold, B. 2006). Recent findings in a field of epigenetics are providing food for thought. Trait variations that are caused by external, environmental factors that switch genes on and off, affecting how cells read the genes, fall under the umbrella of epigenetics.

Do I really understand what the scientists are saying? No, I do not—at least not totally. But I do understand the general meaning of what their studies reveal. Nongenetic factors like toxins in the environment, like what we eat and drink, whether or not we smoke, whether we experience trauma, or harsh conditions can affect the gene expression of our children's children. According to epigenetics, we do have some control over our genetic legacy.

Today, due to the findings of epigenetics, scientists have discovered that a wide range of behaviors, illnesses, and various health conditions have some degree of evidence that links them to epigenetic mechanisms, including most types of cancers, cognitive dysfunctions, respiratory, reproductive, cardiovascular, and many other illnesses. Many of these illnesses are a result of epigenetic processes, brought on by exposure to heavy metals, diesel exhaust, pesticides, tobacco smoke, radioactivity, viruses, bacteria, and basic nutrients.

Did you notice that I mentioned behaviors, not just physical and mental characteristics? That's right—according to more recent studies, epigenetics is reported to have an effect on behavior. Does that mean that there's a fundamental truth to the biblical principle, "The sins of the father are visited upon the heads of the offspring" (Exodus 20:5 KJV). Believe what you will, but in my opinion, science is once again providing a foundation for biblical truths. Wow, looks like all we have to do is live, and we can be sure that some form of epigenetic processing will occur.

PART III

The Third Dimension of Learning: Addressing the Needs of the Whole Child in the School

CHAPTER 9
EQ vs. IQ

WHILE YOUR CHILD IS STILL AT HOME UNDER your care and supervision, you need to decide how you can best prepare your child for life outside of the nest. Are you more interested in developing his intellectual, academic skills like reading and math, or are you more interested in developing his social skills? Well, the truth is, he is going to need both to survive. I'll be honest, all I thought about was my child's ability to do well academically; I wanted my child to get straight As. At the same time, I taught my children biblical principles and tried to guide them to always be honest and trustworthy and kind to others, but I wasn't concentrating on their emotional intelligence; I didn't really have a goal in mind like I did for academic intelligence.

Once my children left the nest, I began to realize that their emotional state would determine, to a large degree, what their life would be like when they had to interact with their peers. I also realized that I would need to teach them more than just being kind to others, because they need to know what to do when others weren't being kind to them. Once I returned to the classroom, I began to understand some things that changed my way of thinking.

Daniel Goleman's *Emotional Intelligence* was an in-depth reading which was thought provoking, insightful, eye-opening, and inspirational (Goleman, 1996). I chose this book as a reference because I began to feel that your social and emotional intelligence is much more important than your IQ, but I wanted more factual information and support from a professional in the field. The sub-title of this book, *Why It Can Matter More Than IQ*, informs the reader that it is not a debate but a fact. The author believes that being "intelligent" is not how much quantitative analysis you can explain but being able to read another person's feelings, control emotional impulses, manage relationships, and empathize; that is being intelligent. He presents his scientifically based convictions about emotional intelligence by commencing with an evolutionary explanation of the human brain, where emotions begin. By examining the growth of the human embryo, we know that the emotional part of the brain, the limbic system, develops before the cortex, the thinking part of the brain.

In addition to developing first, the neural circuitry of the limbic system includes the amygdalae, which are in charge of the fight or flight response. Impulses from this circuitry have the ability to reach other parts of the brain in millimeters per second, determining emotions before reaching the cortex, the area of thinking. This in turn delays the time to make common sense judgments (Littlejohn M., 2011). So, what the heck am I saying? For example, a fourth-grade student becomes so enraged that he cannot partner with his friend. He turns his desk over and runs out of the classroom. Goleman would classify this as a prime example of the amygdalae taking control of the cortex, emotions overriding sound judgment.

Research tells us that emotions are observable in the womb. Rapid eye movement, indicative that the fetus is dreaming, explains the fetus's pleasant or unpleasant facial expressions (Chamberlain, D., 2013). Emotional learning continues with infants and the relationships that develop between them and their parents. Positive interactions with their parents instill trust and a sense that their needs will be met. On the other hand, negative interactions instill mistrust and the feeling that nobody cares. Children learn emotional skills long before they learn cognitive skills. Developing positive relationships is crucial in the first three to four years of life.

As a classroom teacher, I saw incidents daily where emotions hijacked rational thinking. However, not until reading this book did I truly understand the neurological anatomy that explains certain types of behavior.

After presenting visual diagrams of the key components of the brain and their relations to emotions and cognitive learning, the author cites several studies performed by psychologists that back up his unwavering belief that IQ is not a predictor of success in the classroom, nor in life. According to Goleman, IQ contributes about 20 percent to the factors that determine life success, which leaves 80 percent to other factors, like self-motivation, empathy, not allowing stress to overpower the ability to think clearly, and having hope.

The ability to think clearly and how this emotional intelligence skill can be overpowered was one of the topics of interest to me. Why? Because I have witnessed colleagues and myself who have been in a stressed-out state of mind. Now I understand what happens in the brain when people say, "I can't think straight!" The prefrontal cortex executes the working memory; however, this is the part of the brain where feelings and emotions meet. When we are stressed out, the working memory is overpowered, and suddenly, we can't think straight (Teele, 2000). It is so very important that children learn techniques for self-regulating their emotions, and these techniques need to begin in the home if at all possible. I have chosen my favorite technique to share with you, *Calm Down With Take Five Breathing*, which involves using the fingers of the hand to carry out a quiet re-focusing exercise (Childhood 101, 2016).

Figure 9.1 Self-regulation technique

I like this method of self-regulation because it can be done any-where, and it's easy. The deep breathing while focusing on an action helps to balance the body. Children have to breathe in through their noses and blow out through their slightly opened mouths. Once they get the breathing under control, they use the pointer finger of one hand to trace the fingers of the other hand. These are the steps in sequence and more detail:

1. Stretch one of your hands out like a star.
2. Use the pointer finger of the other hand. Start at the bottom of the outside of the thumb and slide your pointer finger

up the thumb, pause at the top, then trace the inside of the thumb to the bottom. Continue tracing each finger, remembering to pause at the top.

3. Now begin the slow, steady breathing. It's important to take deep breaths in through the nose and blow air out through the mouth.

4. Combine the slow, steady, deep breathing with tracing the fingers. Begin with the bottom of the thumb; breathe in as you trace up and breathe out as you trace down each finger. Each breath taken in and blown out counts as one breath. If it's done correctly, five breaths will be taken.

5. If you feel calm, you can stop, but if you don't, repeat the process.

Teaching children techniques like this can mean the difference between success and failure. Like anything else learned, practice makes perfect, so practice, practice, and practice. There are many other techniques available, so explore them and find one that you and your child like.

Many of us believe that your emotions affect your immune system, but I did not truly understand how this works until I read chapter 11 of Goleman's *Emotional Intelligence* and Candace Pert's *Molecules of Emotions* (1997). Goleman directs the reader to the discovery by Robert Ader, a psychologist, who discovered that the central nervous system and the immune system communicate through biological pathways. These pathways interlace the mind, the emotions, and the body, thus dispelling the belief that the brain and the central nervous system are separate entities. Years later, based on the findings of Adler's research, his colleague David Felton and his wife, Suzanne, noticed a direct physical pathway that allowed emotions to impact the immune system. This was a phenomenal discovery. No one had been able to offer any validity to the possibility that the immune cells could receive messages from the nerves. Not only is the nervous system connected to the immune system, but it is a key component for proper immune functions. A few years later, Candice Pert, whose work was referenced in the previous chapter, discovered how neuropeptides are the receptors that unite the brain, glands, and immune system in a network of communication between brain and body. This explains why we really do feel emotions in the throat, esophagus, stomach, and heart. Even though I truly believed that your emotions play a big role in your health, I had to read both of these books to understand the science behind it. I believed it, but I just couldn't understand it; I think I'm a little slow, seriously.

I know, I got carried away and strayed a little off topic, but the role of emotions is so huge, I had to mention how they affect our physical health as well as our social health. Being emotionally stable is a prerequisite for developing good social skills. Being emotionally stable means having the ability to reduce anger and hostility and other detrimental emotions that need to be controlled. Evidence from various studies is suggesting that the power of anger and hostility damages the heart. Studies done by Dr. Redford Williams at Duke University found that being prone to anger was a stronger predictor of dying young than other risk factors, such as high blood pressure, high cholesterol, and smoking. Anger is energizing, even exhilarating, and it is the most difficult mood to control. So how do you diffuse anger? One way to diffuse anger is by picturing things differently. Presenting a situation more positively puts anger to rest, and seeing things from another perspective plays a role in developing resiliency. Another way of deescalating anger is cooling off physiologically with exercise, deep breathing, and muscle relaxation. This helps because it changes the body's physiology from high arousal of anger to a low-arousal state. It is also a distraction. Being able to reframe an individual's state of anger is a skill that only a person with emotional intelligence can perform.

When I think of people who are able to control their emotions, President Obama comes to mind. I'm sure that he has a high IQ, but it is his EQ that makes him a true leader. His ability to laugh about criticism and derogatory comments is indicative of his level of resiliency.

As parents, we have to model this kind of behavior as often as possible. I know it can be difficult, but be aware of your words and actions. As teachers, we have to make time to discuss actions and alternatives to negative situations. Children have to learn how to use their minds to help them realize what's most important, and that is staying happy, healthy, and out of trouble. All of us learned how to read and write in school, but most of us never learned how to sidestep controversy and anger, or develop resiliency. I realize that part of a child's personality is due to his DNA, but don't let that stop you from being the best role model you can be. Practice bullying situations with your child. Practice responses that deescalate mean, nasty phrases.

Make sure you explain to your child that people who bully others have problems within themselves. They need to feel power, importance, and a sense of belonging. Many of them are angry without understanding why. Bullies come from different economic groups, races, and religions. It's been around since the beginning of time. It just seems to have gotten much worse with the addition of cyber bullying. Fortunately, schools are actively addressing this issue by teaching conflict resolution, but it's going to take all of us to combat this deadly trend.

Figure 9.2 Practice conflict resolution

What kind of clever response could you come up with to counteract this type of bullying? This is what I would say: "I know, it's a shame everyone can't be smart and beautiful; I would love to be smart and beautiful, but God made me the way I am, and there's nothing I can do about it." I'm sure you could think of lots of other things to say, but remember, you want to avoid conflict.

CHAPTER 10

Learning in the School Should Be Brain Compatible

*W*ELL, HERE WE ARE, BACK TO THE BASIC CON-
cepts of formal education, what they are, and what they need
to be. Let's begin by answering this question, "What is brain-compatible learning, better known as brain-based learning?" In the past
decade, new brain-imaging techniques have allowed us to observe
the brain while it is learning. The field of neuroscience has produced
a body of empirical data that provides a new understanding of how
we learn. This body of data has undeniable implications in education.

Brain-compatible learning refers to how the brain best learns and
how teaching methods, classroom arrangements, lesson designs, and
school programs should be informed by this latest scientific research.
The body of findings of how the brain learns includes such factors
as cognitive development, how students learn differently as they age,
grow, and mature socially, emotionally, and cognitively, and how certain emotional states can facilitate or impede learning, among many
other findings.

There are specific tenets of a Brain-compatible or Brain-based
classroom that should be obvious upon observing the teacher-student

interaction, in addition to classroom management (Kovalik, S. 2001). The ten most impactful tenets are:

- Emotional engagement, the most important tenet of the brain-based classroom, which occurs when these other standards are met
- A safe, nonthreatening environment (students are allowed to ask questions and make mistakes without ridicule)
- Respect for each student's learning style as well as dominant intelligence
- Lessons integrated with movement and music
- Feeling of empowerment (student jobs and responsibilities that make the classroom experience run more smoothly)
- Novelty (routine provides security, expectations, and normalcy, but doing new and different strategies when introducing new learning experiences improves level of reception and connections)
- Use of previous knowledge and memories to build new skills
- Lessons that are authentic, relating to real-life experiences, especially those that relate to students
- Committed time for teamwork and collaboration
- Freedom of choice (students allowed to make choices within the teacher's guidelines and structure)
- Information provided to students about the brain and how it learns

Let's start with the first day of school in a typical elementary building. As the new students enter the classroom, what would you say the average teacher is thinking? Is she looking at a child on this first day of school and wondering if this child is well behaved or a discipline problem, smart or not so smart?

What if these teachers were practitioners of brain-compatible teaching? What else would they be asking themselves about this student? Remember, now they are thinking like teachers informed by science, dealing with the whole child. They are acknowledging that each child has his own learning style, his own method, rate, and speed of processing, as well as his unique way of making sense of the environment.

Thirty years of teaching experience has shown me that most elementary school teachers notice the emotional state of the children as they enter the classroom the first day of school, which is crucial to the child's future success. However, it has also come to my attention that the higher the grade, the lower the teacher's attention to the child's emotional state. It's probably unfair to say that they don't notice, because I'm sure that many do. It's just unfortunate that circumstances don't permit scrutiny of the whole child at this level.

Once again, I repeat, and science reiterates, you need to look at and address the *whole child* at every grade level. Looking at a child and labeling her or tagging her as undesirable because of what her previous teacher said, without getting to know who she really is, is not acceptable. You just have to expect the best and deal with what you get.

Before we move on, allow me to share this experience with you. As a classroom teacher, I discouraged and paid little to no attention to reports from the child's previous teachers. On that first day of school, I saw each of my students as a successful learner. I drew my own conclusions after I got to know the whole child. Since I didn't know how some students had been labeled, I expected them to do the same work as everyone else, and guess what? In many cases they exceeded all previous teachers' expectations. Imagine the pride these children felt when they didn't get modified work; it developed a sense of determination and a strong desire to succeed. Sometimes that increased confidence is enough to change a child's level of success.

Have you ever given thought to how your students make sense of their environment? As a classroom teacher, have you ever looked at a child on that first day of school and wondered how the child's vision, hearing, balance, or sensory integration was functioning? Did you notice how the child walked into the room with arms and legs moving in opposite directions? Did you notice how he sat at his desk or viewed the screen or board? I must give credit to the teachers who do notice if a child squints when reading or looking at the board, leans to one side when writing, or generally slumps over his desk, or did his previous teacher's words color your perception of the child? I'm sure you notice, but does it register as something that needs more attention and investigation? Regrettably, these characteristics are often overlooked because a former teacher's experiences with a child have influenced your own. You are so preoccupied with the problems you think you are going to have with a particular child that you fail to notice the obvious. In addition to that, teacher training has not stamped these types of characteristics with a priority status. Forget priority status; they are not even addressed in a regular teacher's program. Unless programs have changed drastically, these concepts are presented and examined only in special education programs. After all, there are no grades attached to how children walk, feel, or do anything immeasurable.

It's amazing to me that children do as well as they do, considering all of the baggage that many of them bring with them to school every day. Now imagine a child in a classroom where her teachers don't really know her for the first half of the year, and by that time, her attitudes and study habits have been formed. She functions like the "walking dead," attending classes in the physical state only, with no emotional engagement involved. Classes that could get her attention, like music, art, and physical education, not to mention recess, have been decreased and/or deleted at all grade levels to make more time for test prep and testing. It's incredible that kindergarteners are allowed to be traumatized the first week of school with testing. Anyone who knows and understands children is appalled by the new educational guidelines and stipulations. I know that the average teacher is unhappy about the constant testing and controlled strategies prescribed by politicians who have spent little to no time in the classroom. I've had the opportunity to speak with several kindergarten teachers, but I'd like to quote a kindergarten teacher, from the Winton Woods school district in Cincinnati, Ohio.

Kindergarten *home-living time* used to play a crucial role in the child's socialization process. A special home-life center was an area of the classroom where two or three children at a time could play "house" independently, while the teacher worked with other groups of children. The center was furnished with a kitchen, consisting of a play refrigerator, stocked with play food, a stove with little pots and pans, a sink, a table set with little dishes, a living space with a small sofa, cradle, and highchair with a doll baby in it. Spending time in this center allowed children to interact in a natural way without set goals or expectations. Children learned how to problem solve, share, communicate (it was especially beneficial to the children who knew very little English), and show empathy for one another. Not only was the child's emotional self revealed in this setting, but the part of the child that sometimes goes unseen during academic settings became observable. The teacher would often see a reflection of herself or a parent in the way the children interacted. It provided a window into the world of the children, which informed the teacher in a way that increased her understanding and connection to each individual child. Kindergarten playtime has now been relegated to the preschool and replaced with academics. (A. Byrd, personal communication, 2015)

After all, kindergarteners don't need to waste time playing, learning how to be decent human beings, when they could be learning how to read. This must be what the politicians think. I agree that they need to learn how to read, *but they also need to learn how to get along with each other.*

Don't you think that before policies are set in stone, the individuals who make them should be informed by those who are responsible for enforcing them, as well as those who will be affected by them? It seems as though the concepts of good, sound teaching practices, which have historically been based on the principles of child development, have been trashed and replaced by the principles of high-stakes testing trauma. I'm not saying that we have to be stuck in our old ways and not be enlightened by new findings, but some of those old ways developed some pretty fine individuals.

Some teachers think they are doing a great job because they begin the year by introducing themselves to their students. As part of this introduction, they set rules and expectations that often jeopardize the feeling of a safe environment. This certainly is a necessary thing to do, but what about providing an opportunity for the students to introduce themselves to you and each other? What about allowing them to feel empowered by setting their own rules and expectations? If they don't match exactly what you were thinking, you can add to them or figure out a clever way to modify them. In many cases the rules and expectations they set forth are stricter than the ones you had in mind.

Ideally, every teacher should be on a mission to find out what the strengths and passions are of each child instead of zeroing in on his weaknesses. Teachers should begin the year with activities that promote emotional engagement, activities that are fun and interactive. Students rarely get the chance to talk about themselves in front of an audience. Since this could prove to be embarrassing to some students, they could be given a list of questions to provide guidance to what they say. For example, "What is your favorite color, pet, sport, music? What makes you happy, angry, or sad, and what is your favorite and least favorite subject?" Questions of this sort have no wrong or right answer, because they are relative to each individual. The answers are acceptable because they are judgment-free, while giving you insight into the child's immeasurable parts. Students have reported that this kind of activity was fun to them. They were emotionally engaged while getting to know their classmates and establishing an invisible bond of belonging. The classroom should become their community.

While reflecting on my first teaching experience, back in the days of the cavemen, the '60s, I realized early on just how important this sense of belonging was to classroom discipline and emotional engagement in academics. I realized that assigning jobs and responsibilities to each student encouraged them to function as a community of learners and gave them a sense of control. It became evident that movement and performing arts were beneficial to learning; the emotional impact on the students was obvious. I was teaching in a public school system that had no books for the second-grade class that was located in the basement of the school near the furnace room. These classrooms in the basement were composed of the African American children who had just integrated the school. I could go on about that situation, but that's another book. The point is that I was responsible for teaching these children how to read without reading books, workbooks, or even worksheets of any kind. I was the sixth teacher they had been assigned since the beginning of the school year, and it was now just November. These children were emotionally distraught and in a state of chaos. I had to make a decision quickly.

I decided to forego the academics and get acquainted with my class. I realized that any class that was on their sixth teacher after only three months of school was in emotional upheaval. I had to listen to the children, their stories, their lives, what they did away from school, and find out what moved and engaged them emotionally. I needed to know each child, the whole child, before introducing academics.

It didn't take long before they let me know exactly what turned them on: music, rhythm, dance, and let me not forget food.

I used rhythm and movement to teach sight words and syllabication, rhymes to teach phonics and reading rules, and popular music in conjunction with daily experience charts to teach reading, and dance at recess and ice cream sundaes on Friday afternoons to reward them for being such great learners. My students' first reader for second grade consisted of the words to the Michael Jackson song, "ABC." You cannot imagine how excited they were to play this song and write the words and then read them; it wasn't work to them at all. With the amazing input of movement, music, rhythm, and dance, these children excelled and had fun while learning. Isn't that the way it's supposed to be, even when you have all the materials you need? Just saying.

Don't misinterpret what I am saying. I don't mean that every teacher needs to play popular music as a teaching strategy, but some type of music only enriches the learning experience. What I do mean is that every teacher should have something novel in her tool bag, so that when and if the opportunity presents itself, she'll be prepared. Every teacher should do things to make learning fun.

When I began working on my doctorate, almost fifty years later, I often thought about my experiences in my first classroom and how much success my students achieved while having fun. As part of my doctoral research, I had the opportunity to interview students from different schools in different cities, states, and even countries. Amazingly, when students were asked the question, "What is your favorite subject and why?" they all answered the same way. They liked certain classes because they were fun! They liked the teachers because they made learning fun. Even children in the schools of St. Petersburg, Russia, responded in the same way. Emotional engagement was the foundation for learning that made school fun. Back in the '60s I had never heard of brain-based learning or emotional engagement, but

I did have enough sense to realize what turned my students on to learning. Emotional engagement was and always will be crucial to how the brain learns and remembers.

An analysis of emotional engagement shows that certain criteria need to be met. Movement, music, healthy competition, structured student control of the environment, opportunities for leadership roles, a sense of belonging to a group, and absence of threat are essential in developing an environment founded on emotional engagement. In my experience, the most important of these are movement and absence of threat.

Understandably, allowing students to move or change desks, or do something different from the norm, can cause fear in the hearts and minds of many teachers. To do this successfully, the teacher has to have a structured form of discipline. For example, establish a particular clap that alerts students that an activity has ended. Play music to signify the ending or beginning of an activity. Isn't that more interesting than telling them to sit down and be quiet? Remember this: the brain loves novelty, so any novelty that you can create to help you manage your classroom can make a huge difference in the way your students respond to your expectations.

One form of movement that is nonthreatening to the teacher is called *Brain Gym* by Paul Dennison, PhD, and Gail Dennison (Dennison, 2010). You might have heard of it, for it has gained much popularity in the last ten years. Brain Gym exercises, all twenty-six of them, were designed to integrate body and mind while addressing visual skills, like eye teaming, in order to improve reading, writing, memory, and concentration. It is based on three simple premises:

1. Children naturally learn through movement and play.
2. Learning blocks are the inability to move through the stress, lack of confidence, and uncertainty of a new task. Successful

learning begins with an awareness of this imbalance, followed by experimentation.

3. Learners of any age can come to an impasse. The twenty-six Brain Gym activities "foster the flexibility, eye teaming, eye-hand coordination, and postural alignment that allow learners to thrive in a learning environment and live happily and creatively amid the stressors of modern life."

Brain Gym includes lots of cross-lateral movement, which is great for stimulating both sides of the brain. It also creates positive changes in attention and the ability to focus. It can be done every day and only takes a few minutes to complete. Each of the twenty-six activities addresses a specific classroom-related skill. I have taught Brain Gym moves to my grandchildren so that they can use them in the morning before school and in the evening before homework. PACE is what we usually do because it only takes about five minutes. It represents four of the twenty-six Brain Gym moves. Each of these moves serves a special purpose and is to be done in a particular sequence. These exercises promote a mind-body connection and create a readiness for learning through simple, energizing movements. Doing the exercises of PACE made a big difference by helping my grandchildren develop a more positive attitude toward academics and transformed the somewhat negative task of doing homework into something that's lots of fun.

So, just think about it. If just four simple moves can increase readiness for learning, imagine what the positive impact that using all twenty-six Brain Gym moves could make. Well, as a classroom teacher and vision therapist, who made consistent use of these exercises, I'm here to testify that they did make a huge difference.

The Cross Crawl

ACTIVE

Part I Part II

Hook-ups

POSITIVE

ENERGETIC

Brain Buttons

CLEAR

Sipping Water

The PACE activities are from Brain Gym®: Teacher's Edition, © Edu-Kinesthetics, Inc.; images and descriptions used with permission. Brain Gym is a trademark of the Educational Kinesiology Foundation, BrainGym.org.

Figure 10.1 PACE: Sample of Brain Gym moves (Dennison, 2010)

PACE offers one example of how Brain Gym supports readiness. Begin by sipping water and move counterclockwise through the activities. See HeartsatPlay.com/videos.

Dr. Carla Hannaford, neurophysiologist, author of *Smart Moves* (1995), and a proponent of Brain Gym concepts, writes:

> Cross-lateral movements activate both hemispheres in a balanced way. These activities work both sides of the body and involve coordinated movements of both eyes, both ears, both hands and feet, as well as balanced core muscles ...
>
> When this occurs, both hemispheres and all four lobes of the brain are activated, cognitive function is heightened and ease of learning increases.

The teacher needs to know what kind of behaviors indicate that the child is having problems with perceiving and integrating information. With Brain Gym, most learning blocks can be removed, whether recognized or not.

The exercises are also a great way to quietly wake up the brain and keep it firing. This should be of special interest to adults who spend many hours in boring meetings, trying to stay awake. Think about how many times you've been stuck in a meeting, or presentation, trying to look alert and intelligent, while being bored stiff. You are sitting there wishing you had a drink, or that you were anywhere else. Worry no more; you can inconspicuously do Brain Gym exercises that will wake you up and keep your brain firing.

As an adult, it's difficult to sit still and pay attention for long periods of time, and if you're anything like me, you have little to no energy. Try to imagine our poor children, who have tons of energy, being forced to sit at their desks or tables for hours; they need movement. It doesn't make sense to force them to bottle up all that energy; whether you know Brain Gym exercises or brain-based learning or not, children must be allowed to move with purpose and within structure that is naturally integrated into the lesson plan.

Just to give you an example, during the first week of school, 90 percent of my students named math as their least-favorite subject. I knew that I had to get them emotionally engaged in math as soon as possible. So, at math time, we would spend two minutes on Brain Gym crossover exercises, and then I would put on some "math music," which is music with a good, strong beat. The math exercise leader, chosen at the beginning of the week, would come to the front of the room to lead the class in rhythmic exercises for one minute and a Brain Gym exercise for one minute. Guess what happened? Every student began to look forward to math time. The "hate math" mind-set was being replaced by more positive thoughts about math. By the end of the year, every one of my students loved math. That didn't mean that they were all A students, but it did mean that their minds were open to learning and working to the best of their ability. Those four minutes of music and movement had removed mental math blocks and opened the pathway to critical learning.

As a classroom teacher, you must remember that movement within your structure is crucial; it works best as a planned activity. However, that does not mean that teachable moments where movement would be spontaneous should be excluded. If you can integrate movement into language and reading within a teachable moment, by all means do it. I recall having taught a lesson on *onomatopoeia* in language and being so excited when I realized that the story we were reading provided great examples of it.

Figure 10.2 Examples of Onomatopoeia
(Illustration by Brenda Hunter, 2017)

I stopped reading and instructed the students to let me know that they recognized examples of onomatopoeia by placing their hands around their mouths and making the appropriate sound when it appeared in the story. It took a lot of nerve to do this, but I had to see how it would work; it paid off. The students now had a reason to stay attentive; it was something new and different, and the brain liked it. While having fun, they were able to apply what they had been taught. They learned the meaning of a big, Greek word, as well as a new writing technique.

I bet you are thinking that this movement is not the movement that you had in mind. I know it's much smaller and more subdued, but it's engaging and fun. While movement involving large muscles, and changes in body positions, is very stimulating, any purposeful motion involving any part of the body, as well as the senses, provides new activities and keeps the brain firing.

Last, but not least, students need to have the freedom to make mistakes without ridicule. If you ask a question and the student responds with the incorrect answer, say, "Okay" or "Thank you," and ask if anyone has a different thought. Let them know that you appreciate their participation. If you don't get the answer you're looking for, ask the question in a different way that will lead to the correct answer. Let's face it—sometimes you never get the answer you want, so after a while, give them the answer, but be patient. The most important thing to remember is that you want each student to feel valued and experience *freedom from threat.*

When lessons and activities in the classroom are based on how the brain learns, the child will learn. A great amount of emphasis should be placed on movement, music, rhythm, a threat-free environment, and activities that are new and different, activities that wake the brain up and give it reason to pay attention.

CHAPTER 11

The Brain-Compatible Classroom: Multiple Intelligences and Learning Styles

*I BET YOU ARE WONDERING ABOUT MULTIPLE IN-*telligences and the role this concept plays in a brain-compatible curriculum, and if you're not, you should be (Gardner, 1985). Well, here's the thing. If and when a classroom is guided by or founded on the principles of brain-compatible learning, multiple intelligences would be one of the foundation's cornerstones. Simply put, each child's natural-born intelligence (strength) would play a crucial role in the overall curricular development and be evident in every teacher's lesson plan. Unfortunately, this is too often not the case. The traditional mind-set of what intelligence is has clouded the minds and practices of educators as well as the general population. A child's level of intelligence is based upon scores from standardized tests that are assumed to be an accurate measure of every test-taker, even though they mainly test linguistic and mathematical skills. While it's true that every child needs to know how to read, write, and do math to comfortably survive in this society, it is also true that other intelligences are necessary for a well-rounded individual. Very often the intelligences or skill sets of individuals that are ignored are the ones that society depends on for quality of life.

According to Howard Gardner, there are eight distinct types of intelligence; there were originally seven, but Gardner added Naturalistic to make it eight, and I'm sure that more will be identified in the near future.

- Verbal/linguistic
- Logical/mathematical
- Musical
- Visual/spatial
- Body/kinesthetic
- Interpersonal
- Intrapersonal
- Naturalistic

I know that you are able to pick out three or four intelligences, other than linguistic or mathematical, that make your life enjoyable and well worth living. Gardner's theory of multiple intelligences provides a valuable guide for educators to use for developing curricula that acknowledge as well as nurture the needs and strengths of each individual child. It helps us figure out what the child's learning style is. A child who loves music, rhythmic songs, and rhymes has a musical intelligence and an auditory learning style. Every child is smart to varying degrees depending on the intelligence. Exhibiting strength in one intelligence does not rule out strength in an additional one, or indicate weakness in a different intelligence. Most children have strength or potential strength in more than one method of interacting with the world.

Some individuals have five or six strong intelligences and are amazing to observe. I have personally had the privilege of teaching students who were linguistic, mathematical, musical, spatial, kinesthetic, interpersonal, and intrapersonal. Most children in any typical classroom have overlapping intelligences, which give them the freedom and promise of reaching the majority of students with methods based on linguistic, mathematical, musical, kinesthetic, and spatial intelligences. If you can include the rest, go for it.

Designing school classrooms to allow experiences with a majority of the intelligences should be a prerequisite, or at least the goal of every elementary school district. Obviously, linguistic and mathematical intelligences are addressed; they represent the foundation of every curriculum, but what about the naturalistic intelligence? Years ago, plants in the classroom were very common, and children were given the job of taking care of them. Now when I walk into a classroom, I am surprised to see a plant, and forget about fish tanks or animals to care for. What about auditory/musical intelligence? I am not talking about actual music classes that children have scheduled as one of their specials; I'm talking about the use of rhythm, rhyme, rules put to music, listening to music as a segue into lessons, as well as using music to enhance classroom management. For example, children love responding to instructions that depend on music beginning and ending (i.e.," Everyone should be in their seat when the music stops"). The uncertainty of when the music will stop is almost like musical chairs, but without the disappointment of someone losing their seat and being counted out. At any rate, it's a lot more exciting than being told verbally, "Take your seats, now."

Since the theory of MI represents different mental, cognitive, physical, emotional, and spiritual abilities, teachers need to become adept at using the child's strongest intelligence to get the child engaged, and then by doing so, increase the child's openness to working on the weakest areas of intelligence.

Current research has informed us that intelligence levels can change, because the brain is plastic and the behaviors of the individual can foster this modification. Through strategically planned activities and enrichment, the intelligence of a child can be expanded and developed. If a child's strength is in an area other than language or math, then chances are he will go through school without ever being fully emotionally engaged.

What does all of this mean in student-teacher talk? It means that teachers need to be given the opportunity and guidance to look for and be open to each child's passion, and to the subjects and activities that are exciting to him. A child's grasp of language skills can be enhanced if the teacher understands the importance of providing exercises and lessons that integrate intelligences, as well as senses, so that all students can grow and benefit from them. This becomes difficult when most of the teacher's time is devoted to making sure test material is covered, but it's not impossible. A little extra time spent making a lesson emotionally engaging will pay off with better retention and connection-making.

For example, quite a few of my fourth graders were having a difficult time with the placement of quotation marks in their sentences. They did a little better with identifying the marks as "sixes" or "nines" because using these numbers provided a familiar visual reference. However, they did a whole lot better when I introduced real elbow macaroni to be used in their sentences, because it represented a concrete, visual, tactile experience. Seriously? How did I do that? Well, first of all I had them write their sentences on a large piece of construction paper. Right away I got their attention because this was something new and different from the normal routine. Then they had to identify where the quotation marks should go. After that, they were instructed to glue the elbow macaroni in the spaces where the quotation marks would go. They could now use more than one sense; they could use touch along with vision, which relates to the body/kinesthetic and visual/spatial intelligences. The children with that visual-spatial intelligence loved it, and for the first time that year, they became emotionally engaged in a language lesson. How wonderfully weird is that? Their excitement was contagious; it spread throughout the class and even to the teacher, yours truly. The students with weaker language skills became emotionally engaged and open to new learning that produced new memories.

The key idea to recognize is that the teacher has to be educated enough to be able to identify the child's strongest intelligences as well as the weakest ones, and be on a mission to improve upon the child's weaknesses by using the child's strengths. She has to do all of this without slipping into a pattern of honing in on the child's shortcomings. Let's face it, teachers have to be so special, so brave, courageous, loving, and understanding, and a bit of intelligence never hurts. It would make life so much easier for them if testing were not made the center of the curriculum and education took more cues from science and learning connections.

Well, we've discussed brain-based learning, and multiple intelligences, but what about learning styles, which has been mentioned in conjunction with MI? Gardener's theory of multiple intelligences is based on the research of cognitive psychology and human development, centered on content, while the theory of learning styles is founded on psychoanalysis, and concerned with differences in the actual process of learning. All these concepts are interconnected at a very basic level. Very interesting, but what's the difference? Learning styles are concerned with how one receives, gathers, categorizes, retains, and retrieves information. They represent the methods someone uses to approach and complete a task. These styles are fluid and can change or be modified throughout an individual's life. On the other hand, multiple intelligences are centered on content and products of learning and interacting with the environment.

Learning styles are influenced by a person's dominant intelligence. The level of reception and retention of new ideas, concepts, and skills can be greatly affected by the type of MI used to frame the lesson's presentation. For example, if a teacher wants to present a lesson on language rules, she should present the lesson in a novel way. She should present it in a way that is stimulating to students whose dominant intelligence is something other than linguistic.

You can't even attempt to know the whole child without figuring out his primary intelligences as well as his learning style; the two go hand in hand. The connection between a brain-based curriculum, multiple intelligences, and learning styles is a natural one. It only makes sense that if a child enjoys what he's doing, it's probably because it is related to his strengths or dominant intelligence and so increases his desire to learn.

In summary, his learning style complements his strongest intelligence, or "modus operandi" (method of doing things). After all, learning styles are influenced by MI; how an individual receives, processes, retains, and retrieves information can be greatly affected by his dominant intelligence. In addition to that, the intelligence used by the teacher to present the information can have a positive or negative effect on reception, retention, and retrieval of skills.

It's time for the static thinking of educators to end and be broadened and transformed into thought processes that support twenty-first-century scientific discoveries. It's time for educators and politicians to cross that bridge that connects science and education.

A brain-based classroom is a place where learning is fun because the children are emotionally engaged (Damasio, 1994). *When the brain and the heart are involved, learning is inevitable.*

CHAPTER 12

Hidden Disabilities: Vision Dysfunction

*H*AVE YOU HEARD THE TERM HIDDEN DISABILI-*ties*? Many people have not, so if you haven't, you are not by yourself. Hidden disabilities are defined as disabling conditions that are not obvious or apparent. They can hinder a person's efforts to achieve in school, work, socializing, and more. Examples of hidden disabilities would be major depression, schizophrenia, bipolar disorder, traumatic brain injury, anxiety disorder, vision dysfunction, auditory dysfunction, and sensory processing disorder. When you happen to interact with someone who has a hidden disability, you might sense that something is not quite right, but you have no idea what his or her problem is, and neither does he or she.

In this chapter, I have chosen vision dysfunction to discuss in further detail because it is a hidden disability that affects many children, yet most people have never heard of it. Consequently, it goes unnoticed and is usually never addressed. There are other conditions unknown to the average teacher that affect some children's academic progress, but in those situations, the needs of the children are being addressed due to the inclusion of occupational therapy. Occupational therapists have been placed in schools to meet those special needs.

While occupational therapy is so beneficial, for some children, it's not enough; they need vision therapy as well.

There is a reading crisis in America, and the most prominent reading problem in America is a result of underdeveloped visual skills. Children of this decade are spending hours and hours indoors watching TV, playing video games, and looking at handheld devices as well as laptops and desktop computers. More time is spent with close-up visual activities than time spent playing outside where visual activities support the development of near as well as far vision skills. Have you noticed how many libraries have closed? If it's not technologically charged, it gets tossed aside. If you have a child who likes to read, praise and encourage him.

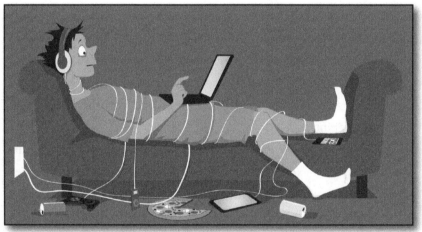
Figure 12.1 Everything technology (thinkstock.com, 2017)

If you are forty years old or older, you know that kids are not doing the same things you did as a child to have fun. Kids spent a lot more time outdoors riding bikes, climbing trees, and playing hide and go seek and other games. All of these activities that you did naturally were developing your visual skills and preparing you for reading.

Vision is a learned skill, like walking and talking. Most of us are born with eyesight but have to learn to use our eyes together as a working team for good vision. In addition to that, our eyes have to be healthy; we have to have good eyesight and good visual skills.

Children suffering from vision dysfunction don't realize they see the printed page differently than others do, so they can't report problems to the teacher. Sometimes words at the end of the sentence float off the page, or words change positions in the sentence, or the last word totally disappears. When things like this happen, children lose their place and their trend of thought, which results in derailed comprehension.

Some children exert a lot of energy trying to keep letters from trading places, words from floating off the page, and other things that occur while reading, and consequently lose interest and the ability to sit still and concentrate. These are often the children who start to fidget and even strike out in frustration. Too often these are also the children who are identified as having attention deficit hyperactive disorder, or much worse than that, a bad brat with behavior issues and lousy parenting.

I also chose vision dysfunction as a topic of discussion because the visual system exemplifies the connectedness of the child's senses. It includes the eyes, brain, and body and is used more than any other sense in the classroom. It is necessary that a child have good, functioning vision to be a good reader, and we all know that every other subject is based on reading skills.

Even math at the first-grade level includes lots of word problems. Math common core testing even includes word problems at the kindergarten level. At some point, all subjects are based on reading comprehension, which requires good vision. In addition to vision's role in academics, years of research and studies have established the strong connection between vision and behavior. Vision problems may interfere with learning and at the same time trigger behavior problems. While this is bad news, the good news is that vision can be trained, and when individuals suffering from vision issues are treated by behavioral or developmental optometrists, learning and behavior can improve.

The average teacher has at least heard of brain-based learning and sensory integration, but at the same time, they have no idea that vision dysfunction even exists. It's so sad and incredible that so many teachers have never heard of this disability, despite the negative effect it can have on the student's ability to read and succeed academically. However, it's not their fault; they haven't been exposed. This is a real problem because people in general, including teachers, think that vision and eyesight are synonymous; they are not. When parents take their children to see an optometrist, they feel that they are following the necessary steps to ensure their child's academic success. When their child's test results indicate twenty/twenty eyesight, the parents are thrilled. Even if the test indicates that glasses are needed, the parent feels satisfied that they have done their job, and they have. They just don't realize that this is only the first step. What they don't know is that an individual can have twenty/twenty eyesight, while suffering from vision dysfunction. Eyesight involves acuity, how the eyes see objects as they reflect light. Vision, on the other hand, takes place in the brain and determines how a person makes sense of his or her environment and navigates through it appropriately. Vision dysfunction has been labeled as "the hidden disability" because it usually accompanies every other disability without ever being diagnosed. The worst part of this situation is that there is help to rectify the conditions associated with vision dysfunction. It has often mistakenly been diagnosed as attention deficit disorder or dyslexia. Conditions such as insufficient convergence, binocularity (eye teaming deficits—eyes do not work together), accommodation (near/far focusing), sensory-motor deficits, eye alignment, eye movement, and reading endurance cause many children to have headaches, blurred vision, loss of place while reading, loss of comprehension, fatigue, frustration, and lack of self-confidence.

An estimated ten million school-aged children have vision conditions that can negatively impact learning, and unknowingly, parents depend on school vision screenings to determine whether their child's eyes are in good working condition. The main goal of the screening is to use the Snellen chart, the twenty/twenty chart, to test for visual acuity and distance visual sharpness, while omitting other crucial visual skills.

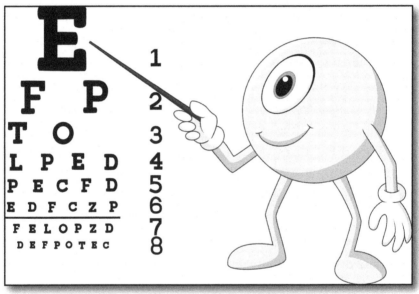

Figure 12.2 Vision testing: Snellen chart (Thinkstock.com, 2017)

Children can pass the vision screening but fail at reading a book. If their child passes the test with a report of having twenty/twenty, or even twenty/forty vision, the parent doesn't see the need for further testing. Twenty/twenty eyesight does not let a teacher or parent know which types of reading problems a child may be experiencing.

It only means that an individual can see letters clearly from twenty feet, which is based on the norm set by what the average person can see. Even if parents were made aware of their child's vision issues, they wouldn't know where to go. The average person has never heard of a behavioral optometrist; I know this from experience. I have asked classroom parents for years if they know what a behavioral optometrist is, and the answer is always the same—no.

So, what is a behavioral or developmental optometrist, and how is he different from a doctor of optometry or an ophthalmologist? Well, I'm so happy you asked. A behavioral or developmental optometrist has postdoctoral training in vision therapy, which is over and above the studies of general optometry. He studies how the eyes and brain function together, how to diagnose issues in the visual process, and how problems with that process can be improved through therapy, to produce a better quality of vision. He believes that visual problems are a result of environmental issues, which may be part of the child's development and/or induced by stress. The ophthalmologist is a medical doctor whose postdoctoral training is in diseases of the eye and eye surgery. The general optometrist, the behavioral optometrist, as well as the ophthalmologist are all prepared to detect diseases of the eye, as well as certain health problems that are indicated by the condition of the eye, which is a very important skill, but both the optometrist and the ophthalmologist usually believe that visual problems stem from generic or biological variations. Consequently, many ophthalmologists discourage parents who want to try vision therapy. When a child is suspected of having vision problems, the parent should turn to a behavioral optometrist (Mischio, 2016).

Having vision screenings as part of school procedure is a good thing. It's better than nothing. Unfortunately, it is not enough, especially for the students identified as having learning difficulties or having an IEP (individual education plan). Having a *functional* vision test can result in changing a child's life forever (Vision Therapy Center, 2016).

Parents, frankly, I must tell you that waiting for your child to get his first eye exam at school is not the wisest thing to do. Having your child visit a behavioral optometrist before the age of three, and again before he begins school, is a good idea. You have no way of knowing that you need over fifteen visual skills to succeed in reading, learning, sports, and even life. Remember that twenty/twenty acuity does not mean perfect vision; it only means great acuity, which is only one of the fifteen visual skills needed for optimal academic success.

The need for a more thorough screening in schools is paramount. Years ago, in 1895, optometrists and ophthalmologists in New York founded the New York State Optometric Association, an organization dedicated to enhancing and improving vision care of the public and promoting the science of optometry. This organization saw the need for a more comprehensive vision school screening. They realized the need to test for vision function, how the eyes work together to perform particular tasks; this includes a lot more than testing for acuity or how the eyes see. The NYSOA (New York State Optometric Association) developed the most noteworthy vision screening battery, which used functional vision screening methods to detect learning-related vision problems. While this screening battery is more complete than the regular school vision testing, it is long and requires a trained optometric overseer, as well as several volunteers. This program is not very cost effective.

Enter VERA (Visual Efficiency RAting), a software program that provides functional vision testing. While detecting many of the children with vision problems, VERA seems to work more effectively when used with children identified as underachievers and/or having behavior problems. The results for using this program have been positive, but widespread use of it has been limited (Gallaway, 2010).

Science has informed us that vision is considered as the dominant sensory system used in learning. Many children suffer from vision problems that are not addressed in normal vision screening. Problems with convergence, accommodation, and ocular motor deficits, not tested for in regular screenings, have been shown to put students at risk for failure in reading and learning in general. This is understandable since children spend a large part of their day doing work that puts stress on the vision system, not to mention the stress put on this system while playing video games, working on computers and texting after school hours.

Are we not listening to the science? Do we not understand it, or are we just ignoring it because addressing it would involve change? I'm not quite sure why VERA or any other functional vision test has not gained popularity. I think that too many educators are stuck in their ways of dealing with academic and behavior issues, but it's not all their fault; their hands are tied, and they can only do so much to fight the powers that be. Consequently, they get stuck on treating the condition instead of treating the cause of the condition. They get stuck on tutoring and generic interventions instead of considering the root of the problem. I realize that teachers are not allowed to diagnose issues, but they could report to parents what they see and where they should go to seek further help. The problem is that they don't know; they have not been taught what the signs really mean. What do you think a functional vision test would discover? It has been reported by the College of Optometrists in Vision Development (COVD) that one of the most common vision disorders that interferes with reading occurs when the two eyes don't work together, in unison, the way they are supposed to when one is reading. It is estimated that over 60 percent of problem learners have undiagnosed vision problems that play a major role in their academic and behavioral issues. Tutoring average students with below-average reading skills, and never seeking the cause, is like pouring water into a bucket with a hole in it. Sounds similar to what doctors do. Just saying.

If teachers were taught to recognize the symptoms, they could alert the parents. They could also include simple, everyday techniques that would enhance learning by involving the students in sensory integrated activities. While teachers are not authorized to diagnose conditions, they can certainly make suggestions and/or give parents directions for getting help; they could suggest that the parents seek information from a behavioral optometrist as well as an occupational therapist. *The checklist below can help determine if a child suffers with vision dysfunction. Investigating this information could change a child's life.*

1. Skips lines, rereads lines
2. Poor comprehension skills concerning reading only, not verbally
3. Homework takes longer than it should.
4. Reverses letters like b and d
5. Exhibits symptoms of attention deficit hyperactive disorder
6. Quickly tires when reading
7. Reads below grade level
8. Avoids reading
9. Eyes water or turn red when reading
10. Tilts head at an angle and holds book close to eyes when reading
11. Poor writing skills
12. Clumsy or awkward at times

There are other symptoms, but if your child exhibits a majority of these symptoms, please seek the professional help of a *behavioral/developmental* optometrist. These issues can be treated with therapy (Vision Therapy Center, 2016).

I recently had an interview with the parent of an eighth-grade student who shared his frustration with me concerning the plight of his son, Will. It offered a perfect example of how teachers respond to children who have learning disorders that are unfamiliar to them. When the teacher is at a loss, the student is at risk and pays the consequences.

This student was obviously quite intelligent. He loved debating sports and issues in the news and displayed a mature sense of understanding of society and people in general, but he also suffered with attention deficit disorder. Will's teacher reported that he was very polite and respectful to her. He was not a behavior problem; he just couldn't pay attention, or stay organized. He lost his pens and misplaced important papers and was easily distracted by almost anything. He would forget to turn in his homework, and even when he did remember to turn it in, it usually wasn't finished or it was carelessly done. Consequently, he was constantly being told that he was not trying hard enough and that he was smart enough to do much better. The possibility of Will being ADD did not cross the teacher's mind because in her mind, children with ADD had behavior problems, and Will was not one of them. Can you imagine how frustrating it must have been for Will to constantly be chastised about something over which he had no control? Will's mother, an educated teacher, suspected that Will had ADD but couldn't get anyone to listen to her. So many of our children suffer from frustration and a sense of futility because they go through school misunderstood, misdiagnosed, or totally undiagnosed. Due to no fault of their own, teachers are undereducated and not fully prepared to address the multiple needs and conditions of our children, and so, our children's academic success is compromised by obstacles that are preventable.

Near the end of eleventh grade, Will's mother and father finally got the attention of the school's new educational psychologist, who recognized Will's symptoms right away. She agreed to test him for ADD; her analysis was correct. Since she was aware that vision dysfunction goes hand in hand with many other disabilities, she referred him to a behavioral optometrist who discovered that Will was also suffering from vision dysfunction. The evaluation revealed that he had an IQ way above average, but his grades had never been indicative of his intelligence. He had been suffering from a hidden disability all of his school life.

This story had a happy ending because Will was from an upper middle-class family and had parents who were able to seek professional help for their child, but what about all the children who get labeled because there is no one to help them? I'll tell you what happens to them; they end up as dropouts and too often end up in jail, or even worse, dead.

Vision dysfunction is not the only condition that can negatively affect the child's academic success. We have all been well informed about the conditions of attention deficit disorder and the continuum of autism, but what about sensory processing disorder, auditory processing disorder, vestibular dysfunction, and persistent primitive reflexes? How many professors of education are informed enough to teach and prepare teachers to address these issues, or have even heard of these conditions? Another condition that can go undetected is auditory processing disorder. At least this is more easily recognized and addressed by a speech pathologist that is usually part of the school staff. Yet, colleges are preparing professionals who will one day be responsible for teaching children and giving them the skills they will need in this world to thrive and be successful. These future teachers, who are in many ways responsible for our future, need to be made aware of every condition that can interfere or impede a child's academic success. While no one expects them to be doctors or therapists, they need to have the ability to recognize the signs and symptoms of these hidden, little-known disabilities. They need all the support they can get, because they are already dealing with the biggest hidden disability of all: the child's family life.

I must add that not all family situations are negative. Some are very positive, and children from those families are easily identified. It's the child who has a troubled, dysfunctional family, which, if unknown to the teacher, should be considered a hidden disability because it can interfere with the child's academic success. Sometimes dealing with the fallout of a dysfunctional family can make other disabilities look like child's play because it's not observable in the classroom and not discernible by the young child.

CHAPTER 13

Hidden Disabilities: Auditory Processing Disorder

*A*UDITORY PROCESSING DISORDER (APD), ALSO known as central auditory processing disorder (CAPD), is a complex problem affecting about 5 percent of school-aged children. These children can't process the information they hear in the same way as others because their ears and brain don't fully coordinate. For some reason, the way the brain recognizes and interprets sounds is negatively affected, especially the sounds composing speech (Billis, T., 2016).

Children with APD often do not recognize subtle differences between sounds in words, even when the sounds are loud and clear enough to be heard. These kinds of problems usually occur in background noise, which is considered a natural listening environment. They have difficulty understanding any speech unless it is produced in optimal conditions.

When children suffer with APD, they are thought to hear normally because they can usually detect pure tones that are delivered one by one in a very quiet environment (such as a sound-treated room). Those who can normally detect sounds and recognize speech in ideal listening conditions are not considered to have hearing difficulties.

However, the ability to detect the presence of sounds is only one part of the processing that occurs in the auditory system. So, most kids with APD do not have a loss of hearing sensitivity but have a hearing problem in the sense that they do not process auditory information normally.

I have included ADP as a hidden disability because you can pass a hearing test and still have it. It can go undetected for so long. Fortunately, most teachers will recognize that there is an issue of some kind, but this usually doesn't happen right away. If the auditory deficits aren't identified and managed early, many of these children will have speech and language delays in addition to academic problems, not to mention low self-esteem and lack of confidence. *Consider the following questions, and if you answer yes to most of them, your child might have an auditory processing problem* (Understood Team, 2016).

1. Is your child easily distracted or unusually bothered by loud or sudden noises?
2. Are noisy environments upsetting to your child?
3. Does your child's behavior and performance improve in quieter settings?
4. Does your child have difficulty following directions, whether simple or complicated?
5. Does your child have reading, spelling, writing, or other speech-language difficulties?
6. Is abstract information difficult for your child to comprehend?
7. Are verbal or (word) math problems difficult for your child?
8. Is your child disorganized and forgetful?
9. Are conversations hard for your child to follow?
10. Does your child have a history of middle ear infections?

APD is an often-misunderstood problem because many of the behaviors noted above can also appear in other conditions like learning disabilities, attention deficit hyperactivity disorder (ADHD), and even depression. Although APD is often confused with ADHD, it is possible to have both. It is also possible to have APD and specific language impairment or learning disabilities.

The causes of APD are unknown, but evidence suggests links to head trauma, lead poisoning, and chronic ear infections. Due to the fact there are many different possibilities, even combinations of causes, each child must be assessed individually. Audiologists (hearing specialists) can determine if a child has APD. Although speech-language pathologists can get an idea by interacting with the child, only audiologists can perform auditory processing testing and determine if there really is a problem.

Some of the skills a child needs to be evaluated for auditory processing disorder don't develop until age seven or eight. Younger children's brains just haven't matured enough to accept and process a lot of information. Many kids diagnosed with APD can develop better skills with time. Once diagnosed, children with APD usually work with a speech therapist. The audiologist will also recommend that they return for yearly follow-up evaluations.

There are five main problem areas that can affect both home and school activities in children with APD (Gavin, M.L., (2014):

- **Auditory Figure-Ground Problems:** when a child can't pay attention if there's noise in the background. Noisy, low-structured classrooms could be very frustrating.
- **Auditory Memory Problems:** when a child has difficulty remembering information such as directions, lists, or study materials. It can be immediate ("I can't remember it now") and/or delayed ("I can't remember it when I need it for later").

- **Auditory Discrimination Problems:** when a child has difficulty hearing the difference between words or sounds that are similar (coat/boat or ch/sh). This can affect following directions, and reading, spelling, and writing skills, among others.
- **Auditory Attention Problems:** when a child can't stay focused on listening long enough to complete a task or requirement (such as listening to a lecture in school). Kids with CAPD often have trouble maintaining attention, although health, motivation, and attitude also can play a role.
- **Auditory Cohesion Problems:** when higher-level listening tasks are difficult. Auditory cohesion skills—drawing inferences from conversations, understanding riddles, or comprehending math word problems—require more complex auditory processing and more advanced language levels. They develop best when all the other skills (processing skills 1 through 4 above) are intact.

Strategies applied at home and school can ease some of the problem behaviors associated with APD. Since it's common for kids with APD to have difficulty following directions, these tactics might help (Educational Psychology Service, 2011):

1. Most children suffering with APD have difficulty hearing in a noisy environment. It's very important to reduce the background noise at home and at school.
2. Have your child look at you when you're speaking.
3. Use simple, to-the-point sentences.
4. Speak at a slightly slower rate and at a mildly increased volume.
5. Ask your child to repeat the directions back to you and to keep repeating them aloud (or to himself) until the directions are completed.

6. When directions have to be completed at a later time, teach your child to write notes, and wear a watch to keep track of the time. Following a household routine along with general organization and scheduling can also be beneficial.

7. It's especially important to teach your child to notice and identify noisy environments, and solve the problem by moving to quieter places when listening is necessary.

Other strategies that might help:

1. Provide your child with a quiet study place (not the kitchen table).

2. Maintain a peaceful, organized lifestyle.

3. Encourage good eating and sleeping habits.

4. Assign regular and realistic chores, including keeping a neat room and desk.

5. Encourage and praise your child; build your child's self-esteem.

6. Be sure to keep in regular contact with school officials about your child's progress.

7. Kids with APD aren't typically put in special education programs. Instead, teachers can make it easier by doing the following: Change seating plans so the child can sit in the front of the room or with his or her back to the window, providing additional aids for study, like an assignment pad or a tape recorder. Allow child to say sentences or read stories into a recording device and play it back so that he can listen to his own voice.

8. Do some research on the Tomatis method as well as the information the forebrain has to offer concerning the sense of hearing, and the auditory process in general.

Acknowledge that APD is real. One of the most important things that both parents and teachers can do is to acknowledge that like vision dysfunction, APD is often unidentifiable. As a result, children can spend years in school without these conditions being diagnosed. Symptoms and behaviors are *not* within the child's control. Developing a positive, confident attitude and healthy self-esteem in a child with APD can work wonders. Children with APD can go on to be just as successful as other classmates. Although some children do grow up to be adults with APD, by using coping strategies as well as techniques learned in speech therapy, they can be very successful adults.

CHAPTER 14

Hidden Disabilities: Sensory Processing Disorder

SENSORY PROCESSING DISORDER (SPD), ALSO known as sensory integration disorder (SID) or dysfunction, is a neurological condition resulting in a child's inability to manage incoming information from the senses and responding appropriately (WebMD, 2016). Some people with SPD may be oversensitive to things like the seams in socks or the sound of a fire engine. Others may be unresponsive; they don't react to anything, not even pain. Some may be uncoordinated and fall down a lot or bump into things. Many are very hesitant to talk to others in addition to avoiding eye-contact when being spoken to. The brain responds to information coming in from the senses in unusual ways. The real causes of SPD are not observable because they reside in the brain. Even though it has not been labeled as a disability, it is misdiagnosed and misunderstood like other hidden disabilities. One of our brain's jobs is to process the input from several senses at once.

While the baby is in the womb, it begins using some of its senses. Once the baby is born, it is able to detect all seven senses, including the vestibular (balance) and proprioceptive (spatial awareness) senses, sometimes referred to as the "hidden senses." For one reason or another, some children have problems processing stimuli from the environment as well as from inside their bodies. If a child is not able to handle multiple sensations simultaneously, the result is that she doesn't know how to respond. For the child with SPD, everyday functions can be very challenging. In early childhood, children with SPD seem to exhibit odd, inappropriate, and even extreme reactions to simple sensory input. This child tends to be labeled as a behavior problem, or having ADHD. So the big question is, "How do you know if a child has this condition?" Well, certain experiences at birth can result in SPD (Jeanie, 2009):

- Premature birth, especially under thirty-two weeks gestation
- Neurological abnormalities like cerebral palsy or missing brain parts
- Developmental delays, including Down syndrome
- Feeding disorder
- Limited tummy time, and crawling
- Exposure to drugs, both legal and illegal before birth
- Genetic predisposition
- Lack of attachment to a caregiver
- Over- or under-stimulating environment

There are three main categories of sensory processing disorder (Kranowitz, 2005):

1. Sensory modulation problems:
   a. Over-responsiveness—avoids certain sensations, seeks less stimulation
   b. Under-responsiveness—may not detect sensations, seeks more stimulation
   c. Sensory seeking, craves constant stimulation

2. Sensory discrimination problems:
    a. Difficulty distinguishing sensations like tastes, smells, or understanding what a sensation means
3. Sensory-based motor problems:
    a. Problems using both sides of the body at the same time
    b. Problems with fine and gross motor planning, and balance

To investigate the possibility of your child having SPD, carefully observe how your child reacts to various sensations. Notice how he responds to loud noises, clothing, and bedding. Is he responsive or nonresponsive to stimulation with toys or tickling? Following are reactions that you can observe as they relate to each sense:

Touch
- Dislikes hugs and may arch back if not held just right
- Dislikes time spent on floor (tummy time)
- Difficult to calm down
- Doesn't put toys in his mouth
- Takes longer to fall asleep, doesn't stay asleep for very long
- Feeding problems
- Irritable while during bath, having diaper changed, or getting dressed
- Sensitive to tags in clothes, seams in socks, or shoes
- Tends to roughhouse, walk into walls and objects, punch things
- Lack of sensitivity to actions that normally cause pain

Smell
- Overly sensitive to smells
- May not recognize dangerous smells like smoke or something burning

Taste

- Picky eater, spits out food with certain textures
- Gags or vomits easily when given certain foods

Hearing

- Fussy or screams in loud environments
- Does not look at person talking to him in spite of normal hearing
- Makes limited baby babbling if any at all

Vision

- Sensitive to the sun and/or fluorescent light, any light
- Does not look at toys
- Does not establish eye contact when spoken to
- Eyes are not able to track a moving object

Proprioception

- Skips crawling, late with sitting up, rolling, crawling, or walking
- Not able to roll back and forth
- Low muscle tone
- Tires easily
- Does not explore body parts like looking at hands, sucking fingers, or playing with toes
- Falls over when turning head to look away

Vestibular

- Poor balance, clumsy, falls down a lot
- Delayed motor skills like creeping, crawling, rolling, sitting, or cruising
- Little endurance for large motor skills

- Low muscle tone, looks and feels soft
- Stiffens up when unexpected movements occur like being quickly lifted into the air

I've attempted to give you a fairly general overview of SPD to make you aware of it, in case you're not already aware, and to help you figure out if your child or family member has this condition. You might look at these lists and think that your child definitely has SPD, or you might look at it and think that while your child does exhibit some of these behaviors, lots of other kids do also. This is what you need to recognize: *If these behaviors interfere with everyday functions, then it's time to at least have your child evaluated.* I wish that I had been aware of SPD when I began my teaching career; I would have handled some situations differently. Now that I am aware of what I'm observing, I realize that I've had lots of opportunities to interact with children who have SPD.

For example, my friend's four-year-old son used to run through the house, screaming when the vacuum cleaner was turned on, or covered his ears when the grandfather clock chimed. One of the older children I tutored, a twelve-year-old, was sensitive to touch. The first time I hugged him to congratulate him on completing a very challenging task, he stiffened and turned away. His mother explained that he didn't like to be hugged. At that time, I was unaware of SPD, so I didn't know exactly what to think. Maybe I had forgotten to put on deodorant. After the mother made that statement, I just knew that this child had a problem, and I hoped and prayed that there was help for him. The thought of a child going through his young life without hugs was very depressing to me. On the other hand, I can't begin to imagine how parents feel when they can't show love through touching, hugging, or kissing their child.

It's wonderful to know that these odd behaviors have been identified and explained. It's even more wonderful to know that this condition can be treated with occupational therapy or sensory-integrated vision therapy, Brain Gym, rhythmic movement training (YouTube), and brain balance centers, to name a few; there are multiple websites and videos that offer information and exercises that can be done in the home that can help the child with SPD problems (Melillo, 2009).

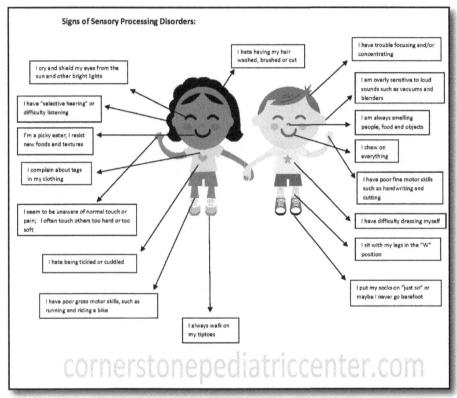

Figure 14.1 Signs of sensory processing disorder.
Cornerstone Pediatric Center (2017)
Specializing in sensory integration, MNRI, vision therapy,
and various neurologically based techniques.

CHAPTER 15

Hidden Disabilities: Gender Confusion

*W*HILE THE EXISTENCE OF GENDER CONFUSION has never been considered a hidden disability (maybe that's because it hasn't been considered), it has been hidden and has been socially and emotionally disabling to those who have to deal with it in their daily lives. The average child with a hidden or unfamiliar disability doesn't realize that he has a condition; he just feels that something is wrong with him. When he can't grasp the lesson being presented the way the other students do, he feels stupid; that's because the way he receives, perceives, and processes information is sensory oriented. He can only make sense of his environment through his own senses, not someone else's.

On the other hand, gender is an obvious classification, or is it? Society makes one think that it is all in the visible anatomy, a simple binary system. From birth, gender surrounds us and transcends us; it determines who we are, how we see ourselves, and how others see and treat us. It determines what toys we play with and until recently, what clothing and colors we wear. Gender differentiation is quickly becoming a topic of extreme interest and discussion. It is now emerging from the shadows of discrimination and misunderstanding into the light of acknowledgment and ultimately acceptance, where it deserves to be.

We are in the midst of a cultural revolution and/or evolution, concerning the binary concept of gender with two fixed options, male or female, and both are founded on an individual's personal anatomy. It's so much more complicated than an "either one or the other" concept.

Biological gender exists along a continuum of anatomical possibilities, but this complex concept is foreign to the majority of people. It includes physical attributes such as external genitalia, gonads, sex chromosomes, sex hormones, in addition to internal reproductive organs. On the other hand, gender *is a* complicated interconnectedness between an individual's biological gender (sex), sense of self or gender identity, whether it be female, male or somewhere in between, and an individual's outward behavior. Putting it simply, Gender is not merely determined by one's physical anatomy (Mandal, A., 2016).

The outward behavior and self-perception produced by the inherent role of gender is influenced by parents, families, schools, churches, and communities, for gender plays a huge role in every phase of an individual's growth and development. The way you learn about gender and respond to it as a child influences how you see yourself and others as an adult.

I vividly recall a family summer trip to Chicago when my son let us know, emphatically, that he would not be wearing a pink T-shirt like the girls; he was only nine years old but obviously had already been imprinted with the concept of gender identification, and it just might have been my fault. This occurred twenty-eight years ago, but just last month I took my grandsons to see the new *Ghost Busters* movie. When I asked them if they enjoyed the movie, the seven-year-old said he didn't like it because "It was an all-girl movie." I couldn't believe my ears. At such a young age, he had preconceived notions about what the sex of the heroes or main characters in a movie should be—male.

Many years ago (1987) as a director of a preschool, it was obvious to me that children as young as three years of age chose activities that were associated with their sex; the boys wanted to play war or some form of fighting, while the girls chose dolls to play with. Their behaviors, for the most part, were typically matched to their sex. Children who naturally fit into these clear-cut categories have no reason to question what gender actually means. The division of sex makes perfect sense to them. But what about the child who anatomically looks like a boy, but only desires to play with dolls like the girls? This happened in my center.

The preschool teacher thought this was absurd and tried to guide him to play with the same toys the other boys were playing with, but to no avail; he continued to work his way back to the dolls and female dress-up clothes. At three years of age, none of the other students seemed to care; at least they didn't tease him or make comments to the teacher. This scenario could have taken place this year. I have personally observed teachers redirecting students' activities and expressions to fit their outward appearance. I am not criticizing them for this, because they are just not informed. I expect this to change in the near future.

As children age, these kinds of experiences have to be more and more confusing. At the age of three, it's not such a big deal for other three-year-olds, but at the age of twelve, a male student choosing to play with typically girl stuff, surely would spark a conversation, even ridicule and bullying. Unfortunately, we've seen too many cases of students being bullied about their gender identification and then committing suicide when the emotional load got to be too much to handle.

Students dealing with gender confusion or a crisis of any kind are at risk of failing to fulfill their academic potential. They suffer with negative self-thought like the students who have hidden disabilities; they know that something is wrong but have no idea what the problem is. The emotional dimension of that child is tainted in a way that can negatively affect learning. If a parent, teacher, or any adult in charge of this student's care shows gender bias with words or actions, the child will suffer the consequences.

Teachers, if you are not already aware of your thoughts and the words and phrases you use with your students, you must become metacognitive. Notice what you think and say. Telling a boy to "man up" might feel like an impossible feat as well as a put-down to some male students. I have actually said this to one of my male students who seemed to cry about everything. I thought I was doing the right thing; expressing sympathy for him only made him cry more. I never once considered his gender makeup. I did consider everything else, like how he was treated at home, was a parent in jail, did a parent recently die, did he have a hidden disability that made him feel stupid or inferior, but never anything related to his gender.

I know how this sounds; I am showing my gender bias by inferring that he was acting like a girl. But that is what I was thinking, because that is what I heard all my life—"Boys don't cry; only girls are cry babies." By the way, I no longer feel that way; I appreciate a man who is strong and secure enough to be able to show emotions with tears.

Growing up, I heard people making fun of boys who acted like girls. They were called derogatory names like "sissy, queer, fag or faggot, and he-shes" out loud and to their faces. I never called anyone a name like that, but I laughed with the crowd when it happened. I knew in my heart that it was wrong, and even then, as an eleven-year-old, I felt so sorry for the child under attack. When I think about how painful of an experience that must have been for a child to be made fun of for being the way he was born, it makes me cry. It's almost like being made fun of for being born black. No one can predetermine their color, race, level of intelligence, physical appearance, or sex, and should never have to suffer emotional destruction caused by characteristics over which they have no control.

Most of us have these biases because they are systemic to our society and culture. What's important is that we examine our hearts and minds and be honest with ourselves about the biases that exist within us; only then can we make a concerted effort to change or at least modify our way of thinking and acting toward others that are different from us.

Gender, in this society, constitutes a fundamental representation of who each individual is. The norm is that individuals are either male or female, and if they do not fall into this norm, they will face innumerable challenges. Even those with slight differences stand to experience much difficulty.

Students are not the only ones without a clue to the complexities of gender expression. Parents and teachers are also clueless. Unless you are the parent of a child born with no visible sex organs, or born with both male and female sex organs, you would probably not give this topic a second thought. This level of ignorance has to be addressed. Hopefully, the following explanations and definitions will be somewhat enlightening, or at least provide food for thought.

I am not a scientist, but I read a lot and try to educate myself for better understanding and tolerance of conditions that members of the human race live with every day. Teachers, please do some research; become informed.

Humans and other animals have an XY sex-determination system. Humans have forty-six chromosomes, including two sex chromosomes, XX in females and XY in males. During conception, the mother's egg provides an X chromosome and the father's sperm provides either an X or a Y chromosome to the zygote (the egg fertilized by the sperm). If the father supplies another X chromosome to the mother's X chromosome, a female is the result. If the father supplies a

Y chromosome to the mother's X chromosome, then the XY combination results in a male. However, the determination and development of the individual's sex is a little more complicated. Having a double X chromosome pattern can produce a male if the gene expression is not what it should be. It is also possible, due to a genetic defect, for a female to have an XY chromosome pattern with testes and no uterus but identifies and sees herself as a female. If this isn't mind-boggling enough, other gene defects exist in XY people that can result in them having ambiguous genitalia, which make them impotent or sterile.

Hormones, in addition to genes play an important role in sexual differentiation and identification (Mastrangelo, J. 2014). If your body doesn't get the right hormones at the right times, things can go in unexpected directions. It can lead to a condition of Intersex, when the XX female has male characteristics on the outside. When an individual is an XX (female) but has too much testosterone produced during fetal development, it can produce both male and female characteristics. The opposite can happen too; an XY (male) can look completely female on the outside.

Just recently, I have been informed by individuals who were victims of childhood molestation, that as a result of this, they experienced *gender confusion*. They felt guilty in some cases because they knew something was wrong but physically enjoyed it, so were ashamed and afraid to tell anyone. One of these individuals, married with children, shared with me that after thirty-six years of questioning and emotionally struggling, the only thing that cleared her mind was prayer and God's divine intervention. Some victims never get help or come to grips with this traumatic experience.

I cannot imagine the pain and confusion involved in looking at yourself in the mirror every day and seeing one sex, while going to bed every night feeling like the opposite sex. I can't imagine how it feels to look like a boy, but have a female brain or vice versa. It's impossible for anyone not afflicted by gender confusion to fully appreciate the plight of those who are.

With new scientific findings describing the complexity of gender identification and expression, new terms and descriptors are developing:

- **GLBTQI**: An acronym that stands for gay, lesbian, transgender, questioning, intersex
- **Gender Identity:** One's innermost concept of self as male, female, both, or neither
- **Gender Expression:** How people display their gender identity through their behaviors, physical expression that is not necessarily indicative of sexual orientation
- **Transgender:** Used as an umbrella to describe anyone whose identity behavior falls outside of stereotypical gender norms.
- **Sexual Orientation:** Being sexually attracted to a specific *gender*
- **Cisgender:** Refers to people whose sex assignment at birth matches their gender identity
- **Gender Fluidity:** Conveys a more flexible range of gender expression; could be either or.

In the near future, elementary school curricula are going to include subjects on gender identity. We must make sure that our teachers are informed by science about the spectrum of gender, so that they can better understand the psychological and emotional state and needs of every child, and thus be able to more effectively teach the whole child.

The state of Washington is one of the first to include standards addressing gender bias as part of their curricula. Washington State's health education glossary defines gender as a social construct based on emotional, behavioral, and cultural characteristics attached to a person's assigned biological sex (Family Policy Institute, 2016).

Their definition of biological sex is based on chromosomes, hormones, and internal and external anatomy. Gender expression is defined as "the way someone actually expresses their gender."

By third grade, students will be expected to explain that gender roles may vary and understand that it is important to treat others with respect regarding gender identity. By the end of elementary school, students will be expected to "understand the range of gender roles, identity, and expression across cultures." I expect that sooner, rather than later, more states will follow suit.

We must be both compassionate and wise. In order to come to grips with this possibility, we must become educated and aware of gender differences. With all of our individual uniqueness, we are all part of God's creation, some less perfect than others, but all deserving of love, acceptance, and respect.

CHAPTER 16

The Role of Diet and Water in Academics and Behavior

*M*ARK HYMAN, MD, IS A VISIONARY IN THE FIELD of medicine and has been practicing and promoting a cutting-edge healthcare concept known as functional medicine. It's a patient-centered (vs. disease-centered) approach that focuses on identifying and addressing the root causes of chronic health challenges as opposed to merely treating symptoms. Functional medicine also incorporates nutrition and changes in lifestyle routines, rather than relying exclusively on pharmaceutical and surgical interventions (Hyman, 2008).

With the epidemic of children coming to school without having had breakfast, in addition to those who have had cookies, cupcakes, or sweetened cereal to start their day, it's amazing that they are able to learn anything. I suppose that having something in your stomach is better than having nothing, but having too much sugar in your diet can cause your body systems to go haywire.

Dr. Hyman reports, like many practicing nutritionists, that most Americans are living out of harmony with their natural biological rhythms, because the small molecules that help keep your body in balance have lost their rhythm.

These molecules—the hormone-messenger molecules of the endocrine system and the neurotransmitter-messenger molecules of the brain and nervous system—are involved in almost every function of the body, and they are critical to our well-being.

All of our hormones and brain-messenger chemicals must work together in a finely orchestrated symphony to keep everything in balance. For example, the hypothalamus and pituitary glands in your brain are the command-and-control centers for all the endocrine (hormone) glands. They send signals to distant parts of the body to control everything from your stress response through your adrenal glands, your blood-sugar balance through your pancreas, your thyroid hormone via your thyroid gland, and function through your reproductive organs. They also control growth, sleep, mood, and much more.

Imbalances or disturbances in any one of these interconnected systems can influence the way our brains function and lead to everything from depression and dementia to anxiety and attention deficit hyperactivity disorder (ADHD). They also are linked to two other major epidemics we currently face: obesity and inflammation. These conditions don't just pop up overnight. They have their beginnings in childhood. Say what? I thought mine popped up last year.

Historically, people ate the equivalent of only twenty teaspoons of sugar a year (exclusively from fruits, berries, tubers, and such). These days, each of us eats on average, about fifty teaspoons a day. There's absolutely nothing in our genetic makeup that could have prepared our bodies to handle this kind of traumatic change, especially when you combine it with the other health-altering changes that have become our natural way of life.

It's frightening to really think about how our children eat and how many hours a day they spend sitting around on their phones, iPads, laptops, or watching television. If something is not a technological device, they have no use for it. Too many of them live a lifestyle that is sedentary and lacking both a healthy diet and adequate physical activity.

Figure 16.1 Sugar addiction starts way too early. (Brenda Hunter, 2017)

Our diet of low-fat, highly processed and refined foods causes the body to pump out more insulin, which, in excess, happens to function as a pro-inflammatory substance.

Eventually, we become resistant to all this excess insulin in our blood, just as we would become resistant to a drug. The body needs more and more of it to do the same job it once did with far less. So our insulin-production system spirals out of control, pumping ever more into our bodies, which then become inflamed and metabolically imbalanced. I personally know this to be true. I thought I was allergic to sugar because after eating lots of sweets, my leg and arm muscles would get sore. Now, I get it.

And what is all this insulin saying to the rest of our body? It's rushing through our bloodstreams spreading the message that we are starving. The result: We start craving foods with high sugar content, the very same foods that caused the problem in the first place.

Think about this when you are getting ready to reward your child with candy. I'm not saying that children should never get to eat candy. I'm just saying that you should not make sweets the center of the rewards process. Too much sugar increases the production of insulin, causing unhealthy results.

Here is what too much insulin really does to your body, your brain, and your health: (The Insulin/Cancer Connection, 2016, 10 Ways to Balance Blood Sugar Naturally, 2014).

- Insulin determines how much fat the body will store.
- Insulin levels, when high, increase your appetite for sugar and refined carbohydrates.
- Insulin increases inflammation and ages your brain, leading to what is being called type 3 diabetes—also known as Alzheimer's.
- Insulin increases LDL ("bad") cholesterol, lowers HDL ("good") cholesterol, raises triglycerides, and increases your blood pressure. Insulin resistance causes 50 percent of all reported cases of high blood pressure.
- Insulin stimulates the growth of cancer cells.
- Insulin leads to depression, panic attacks, anxiety, insomnia, and ADHD.

Here are some suggestions for rebalancing insulin, through nutrition and through your lifestyle: (10 Ways to Balance Blood Sugar Naturally, 2014):

- *Give your child fruits and as often as possible.* This source of carbohydrates, like carrots, sweet potatoes, and beets, helps balance blood sugar.
- *Try to include protein with each of your child's meals.* Start off the day with protein—nuts or nut butters, eggs, a protein shake. It jump-starts your metabolism and helps to prevent overeating throughout the day. Chicken and fish also provide a good source of protein.
- *Eat frequently.* Check with your child's school to see if they provide snack breaks during the school day. Eating small amounts throughout the day speeds up your metabolism. It is very important for your child to have three meals and a couple of snacks every day. Most important to blood sugar level is that your child have three solid meals daily.
- *Build and maintain muscle.* Your biggest metabolic engine is your muscle mass—basically, this is where your metabolism lives—so use it or lose it. Try to make sure that your child gets outdoor, large muscle exercise at least two or three days a week. Every day would be ideal.
- *Deeply relax daily.* Teach your child how to sit quietly, breathe deeply, or meditate, which includes yoga. Cortisol, the stress hormone, increases blood sugar and appetite, and causes weight gain around the middle, all of which promote insulin resistance.

Experience this, and you'll be experiencing functional medicine in action. It's really about harnessing the power one has to reset metabolism and restore the body's natural balance simply by stopping the things that interfere with good health, and by doing the simple things that empower the body to do what it is designed to do, heal itself.

Many of these questions are more relative to the teenager, but if your child answered yes to a majority of these questions, chances are his body is out of balance.

The real concern about diet is the effect insulin production can have on inflammatory response to injury or infection. Chronic inflammation, slowly destroys our organs, compromises our ability for optimal functioning, and leads to rapid aging (Mercola, 2001).

After all, you don't want your child looking like Benjamin Button, do you? Just kidding.

Common treatments such as anti-inflammatory drugs (ibuprofen or aspirin, for example), or steroids like Prozac, are prescribed to treat aggressive behavior and debilitating mental health. The research behind this indicates that there is a correlation between sugar, inflammation, and aggressive, overactive behavior. According to Moises Velasquez-Manoff, a science writer, a third of all the documented cases of children with autism seemed to be the result of inflammatory responses that occurred while the child was in the womb. If the mother experiences food allergies or intolerances, the body responds as though it's under attack with an inflammatory response (Manoff, M.V. 2013)

For many of us, refined sugar, sweets, and breads are not broken down and cause our bodies to react as though a foreign substance had been ingested. This reaction is characterized by inflammation. A chain reaction can occur, which makes for a vicious cycle. It begins with eating sweets. The body reacts to substances that cannot be properly broken down. It releases stress hormones and sugar from the cells, which provide the energy it needs to fight back. The increase of blood sugar level along with the increase of dopamine, the reward neurotransmitter responsible for addictive behavior, results in craving sweets. This cycle continues to produce inflammation, which has been linked to many of the disabilities affecting our children.

I was aware that there is often a connection between consuming too much sugar and aggressive, overactive behavior but didn't understand the science behind it; now it makes more sense. I understand why Prednisone, an anti-inflammatory, is prescribed to people who need to calm down.

I was amazed to find out how many teachers, students, and pets were taking Prozac to decrease aggressive behavior. Seriously? Did I say pets? Yes, I did. Some of you who do not have dogs might not believe me, but I know for a fact that my neighbor's dog, a Jack Russell, took Prozac on a regular basis; he needed it too. Allow me to share this story with you.

One day, when my grandchildren were visiting and playing in the front yard, my neighbor brought the dog over to see them. I stopped washing my car for a minute to talk to my neighbor when he realized that his dog was missing. We searched the front and backyard, but the dog had disappeared. Suddenly my grandson yelled, "There he is, sitting in your car!" I had left my car door open, and he had jumped in. He was sitting behind the steering wheel of my car with his paws on the steering wheel, as though he were ready to drive off. In the case of the dog, the medicine was being taken to make him calmer.

Okay, I'm going to repeat myself. I want you to hear this. I personally know that a lot of the pain I experience is due to the level of inflammation in my body caused by the production of insulin in response to the amount of sugar I consume every day; I am a "sweets-a-holic" (my term for someone addicted to sugar). Taking a comprehensive approach to reducing inflammation at its source is one of the most important things that I or any of us can do to support the core systems of the body. Limiting the sugar in your child's diet will provide a foundation and one of the cornerstones to good health.

In addition to that, if your child is exhibiting overactiveness, aggression, or negative behaviors in general, he might be suffering from what I call the sugar syndrome. Just try reducing sugar and gluten; it just might make a change for the better.

In fact, the future of medicine may no longer have specialties like cardiology or neurology or gastroenterology but a new specialty like inflammology, which would focus on the root causes of disease. In the meantime, it's up to you to keep a close eye on your own addiction to sugar and to take the steps (like those described above) that will keep that addiction from raging out of control.

To help you remember how very informative and important all this is, allow me to summarize what my husband's visiting nurse had to say. She used an analogy that explained a very fundamental biological reason to reduce sugar consumption. She explained it like this to my diabetic husband: At birth, your pancreas, the organ in charge of insulin production and breakdown of sugar, is like a car engine. It is filled with a limited amount of gas, or beta cells, at birth, that have to work for you for a lifetime. When you eat sweets and carbs, you put those specialized cells to work. If you take care of your body's engine by watching the amount of sugar and simple carbohydrates you consume and do not overwork it, those beta cells will last. You can probably make it through life without developing sugar diabetes. On the other hand, if you make the pancreas work too hard for too long, you will use up all those beta cells, and like an engine, it will eventually run out of gas or wear out. This results in the need to provide a different source of insulin, which is indicative of diabetes.

Finally, it took an analogy comparing his pancreas to a car engine to get his attention. Maybe this is an analogy that should be used for all men. Just saying.

One other point that needs to be made clear is that children need to drink water throughout the day. Drinking water and brain function are integrally linked. Lack of water to the brain can cause numerous symptoms, including problems with focus, memory, brain fatigue, and brain fog, as well as headaches, sleep issues, anger, depression, and many more. According to Dr. Corinne Allen, founder of the

Advanced Learning and Development Institute, brain cells need two times more energy than other cells in the body. Water provides this energy more effectively than any other substance. I have heard people say that they get plenty of liquids by drinking juices and sodas, but this is not equal to pure water. You cannot get the same level of hydration drinking alternate liquids.

Over 70 percent of your body is composed of water, and every function in the body is dependent on water, including the activities of the brain and nervous system. Since children are very active, they lose many ounces of water every day through sweating, breathing, and eliminating wastes.

Here's the thing. It is important to drink plenty of water throughout the day for optimal brain function because *water gives the brain the electrical energy for all brain functions, including thought and memory processes, and your brain does not have any way to store water.* When your body loses more water than you are replacing, dehydration will kick in and brain function will be affected.

Dehydration causes your brain to shut down and not run at full speed. Some of the mental symptoms of dehydration include brain fog, afternoon fatigue, focus issues, depression, anger, emotional instability, exhaustion, headaches, sleep issues, stress, and a lack of mental clarity and acuity. Not only that, dehydration can cause your body to actually shut down and your brain to lose consciousness.

If you're tired of hearing about all my experiences, I'm sorry. I just want you to know that usually, when I stress the importance of something, it's because I've personally experienced it. I can remember getting Montezuma's revenge while visiting Mexico. After suffering with vomiting and diarrhea for twenty-four hours, I passed out from dehydration. I fell facedown, hitting a concrete floor. I am blessed to have not been seriously injured. I know now the importance of staying hydrated. I know that this was an extreme case of dehydration, but it provides evidence of how important it is for your child, our students, to drink water throughout the day.

Studies, while not conclusive, have shown that if you are only 1 percent dehydrated, you will most likely have a decrease in cognitive function. If your brain drops 2 percent in body water, you may suffer from fuzzy short-term memory, experience problems with focusing, and have trouble with math computations (Hutchinson, 2016).

Daily hydration will not only help with better thinking, but it *can also help prevent attention deficit disorder in children* and adults. Water provides essential energy to the brain, keeps the nerve signals firing, delivers nutrients to the brain, and removes toxins. We need to be drinking enough water daily to keep the brain fueled and energized for optimum function (Facts are Facts, 2017).

To start your child's day off right for optimal brain function, it is recommended that when she wakes up, she should drink a glass of water. Yes, I know what that means; she'll have to find time to potty before going to school, or as soon as school gets started, but the inconvenience is worth the increased brain activity. Bottom line, if you want your child's brain to function well, receiving and sending signals to the rest of her body, make sure she drinks the water she needs.

As a retired classroom teacher, I know that you have scheduled bathroom breaks and that if children drink water all day, they will have to "go potty." Well, what can I say? Their brains need water to function at their best. So, teachers, please compromise with your students; allow individual breaks within reason. If you as a teacher are not doing this, you need to figure it out. Once the novelty wears off, your children won't ask to go to the bathroom every five minutes.

CHAPTER 17

Education Courses Need Tweaking

*E*VERY COLLEGE PROFESSOR WHO IS RESPONSIBLE for preparing students to teach in elementary and high schools needs to be required to attend workshops and take classes for credit that teach how the whole child is interconnected from the womb to the school. He needs to be challenged to prepare future teachers using best practices, which should certainly include brain-compatible learning. During my years of post-graduate work in education, I learned that most of my professors had never taught in an environment that they were teaching me to manage. How does that work?

My experiences as a doctoral student in educational leadership opened my eyes to the lack of connectedness between education and the science that should be a source of guidance and information for learning. Even though the research behind brain-based learning had been reported and written about for a few years prior to my start date, my department of education knew nothing of it, not even enough to mention it. In spite of the fact that I was a lowly classroom teacher, and a passionate researcher, I felt it was a concept that needed to at least be shared so others would be aware and could come to their own conclusions, but my suggestions to look into this theory were totally rejected and looked upon as ridiculous. My studies, which were supposed to prepare me for educational leadership, should have included information on the concepts of how the brain learns, how to provide a classroom environment led by emotional engagement, the importance of understanding sensory integration, as well as hidden disabilities like the retention of primitive reflexes, vision dysfunction, and vestibular dysfunction, and the role they can play in a student's academic demise.

The knowledge of brain-based learning moved me in such a passionate way, that I decided to make it the focus of my doctorate. Consequently, I had to be advised by a professor in the Cognitive Psychology Department, since that department was involved with the latest scientific findings on brain-based learning. It seemed so ridiculous to me, but it turned out to be a blessing in disguise. It allowed me to get involved with the neurology of how the brain functions. I was actually able to join neurologists in the university's school of medicine to observe children being given fMRIs (functional magnetic resonance imaging that measures brain activity according to changes in blood flow and oxygen levels), and watching how the brain responds to different stimuli was incredible and unforgettable. It only makes sense to me that an educational leader needs to be as knowledgeable as possible, especially when children's academic success depends on it.

I realized that many teachers, including yours truly, were already doing many of the things in the classroom that were compatible with how the brain learns. I was using movement, music, and even dancing to emotionally engage my students. Of course, I didn't think of it as getting them emotionally engaged; I just wanted everyone to learn while having fun. I gave them choices and jobs to empower them; I just felt it was the right thing to do. I was thrilled when parents told me that their children wanted to come to school, even if they were sick. However, when they actually did that, it wasn't such a good thing.

The strategies many teachers have been using for years have been successful; there just wasn't any science to back it up. Teachers have been using some techniques that will stand the test of time; they work no matter what. Then there are others that need to be discarded. I know that many teachers *intuitively* planned lessons that would be considered appropriate for a brain-based curriculum because they felt it was the best way to teach, and they were right.

In spite of all the emotional engagement, brain-based activities, and before and after school interventions, I realized that there were certain students that continued to have problems, mainly with reading and writing, which means that they would end up having problems in every other subject, even math. This was very frustrating to me, and I knew I had to find the answer. I asked God to help me.

What in the world could be the problem? Was I forgetting something important that I had learned in school? It was so conflicting because these were bright students. They were great verbal communicators. In fact, they talked too much. Because of their verbal skills, they were automatically presumed to be good readers, but they weren't. There was a missing piece to this academic puzzle.

My first inclination was to have these bright students with poor reading skills tested for dyslexia. I said to myself, "That's what the problem is." However, I was wrong; the test results were negative. I decided that this situation needed research and a lot of prayer. A few days later, while doing my daily research, I found an article about vision dysfunction and the havoc it plays on a child's academic success. As I examined the characteristics of vision dysfunction, I couldn't help but notice that some of these same characteristics were identical to what I had observed in my own students. Why did this suddenly seem familiar to me? Then it all started to come back; I remembered my past experiences in the Chicago Public School System.

Okay, here's the story. After my first teaching experience in

Chicago, I applied to teach with TWO, The Woodlawn Organization's experimental schools program. Schools that were located in one the most disadvantaged areas of Chicago were chosen to be part of this program. Since I had unknowingly applied to teach at the elementary school associated with the program, I was invited to be an experimental teacher and gladly accepted. I had no idea how dangerous and wonderful it was going to be. Let me just say that working in this program was a blessing to me and my future students.

I volunteered to work after school with a revolutionary new program at the Plano Child Development Center. (How could I have forgotten my experiences with Dr. Johnson and Dr. Moore? These two men changed my life.) What I learned and practiced while in their center was subconsciously impacting my everyday teaching strategies, thirty years later. What an epiphany! At a conscious level, I had forgotten all about the great developmental optometrists, but what I had learned was all imbedded in my long-term memory. It seemed natural, and it wasn't difficult to apply some of the techniques I had learned to address the more common conditions like insufficient convergence, poor accommodation, and tracking. Thank God!

These developmental, behavioral optometrists, Dr. Robert Johnson and Dr. Henry Moore, were the directors of the Plano Child Development Center (Chicago, Illinois), where children received therapy for vision dysfunction. These doctors realized that bright children were failing at reading and not achieving at an optimal level because of the existing conditions unknown to their parents or teachers; Dr. Johnson and Dr. Moore decided to do something about it. They opened a clinic designed to provide integrated vision therapy to students who were suffering academically due to undiagnosed problems with their vision. That center, by the way, was and still is not-for-profit. These doctors charged their clients just a portion of what should have been charged for their professional services. Their mission was to help children succeed, not make money. After all these years, this center is still not-for-profit and functioning today under the leadership of Dr. Stephanie Johnson Brown, the daughter of the late Dr. Robert Johnson. The work of these developmental optometrists has changed the lives of hundreds of Chicago's students and continues to serve those who are in need of help, whether they can afford it or not.

Larry Fitzgerald, the NFC wide receiver for the St. Louis Cardinals, is the grandson of Dr. Robert Johnson and the nephew of Dr. Stephanie Johnson Brown. During several of his pre- and post-Super Bowl interviews, Fitzgerald gave his grandfather, Dr. Johnson, the credit for making him such a great receiver. He reported that the vision therapy that his grandfather prescribed for him made the difference. He also shared that he received this therapy because, like so many other students, he had a vision problem that was making it difficult for him to pay attention in school. He completed his vision therapy under the guidance of his aunt, Dr. Stephanie Johnson-Brown, who now serves as the executive director of the Plano Child Development Center.

Figure 17.1 Larry Fitzgerald, wide receiver of St. Louis Cardinals, catching football. (Getty Images 2013)

After I moved back to Cincinnati from Chicago, I never heard another word about vision dysfunction and the therapy for it until reading that article. It mentioned the work of Dr. David Muth, behavioral optometrist, who was practicing in Glendale, Ohio, a suburb of Cincinnati. I was so excited to find out that vision therapy was still being practiced. I immediately began working with Dr. Muth, who helped me understand the need to include sensory integration exercises in the vision therapy process. I knew then that I had found the missing link, the missing piece of the puzzle of why in spite of all the brain-based things that you do in the classroom, there are still some children who struggle. Wow, it was clear to me that if one of the senses was malfunctioning, with the exception of the most primal ones, smell and taste, then a piece of the child would be in disarray. This would interfere with the well-balanced, successful learning process. So, how do you teach the whole child when one of his parts is out of order?

Well, this is how you do it: you figure out how to reach each child at an emotional level and proceed to teach him as though all parts were in good working order. You use his strengths to strengthen his self-confidence as well as his weaknesses. When a child develops a sense of accomplishment, a positive attitude toward learning emerges and becomes the catalyst for overall improvement. Then you do your best to find the cause or source of the weakness. Teachers, if you don't know what's going on with some of your students, do some research and then talk to an occupational therapist.

I am so thankful that God led me to follow the focus of brain-compatible learning because it opened my mind to so many new concepts that should be a part of every teacher's tool box. It provided the path for me to understand what is meant by the term *the whole child* and hidden conditions that so many children, parents, and teachers have to deal with on a daily basis. Inadvertently, I was reintroduced to an important, life-changing set of skills that I had learned in the past. My reconnection with the existence of the hidden disability, vision dysfunction, would change my life, as well as the lives of many children.

I shared this true story with you because I want you to understand my passion for children and my desire to do the best I can to help every child succeed. I also want you to know that this is what most teachers desire, but not many of them have had an experience like mine, one that introduces them to a whole new world of hidden disabilities. This was great for my education, but what about the student teacher who hasn't had this kind of experience? How can they gain such useful information? They should be able to acquire this kind of information from the Education Department in the college of their choice.

Universities need to equip their colleges of education with studies that represent best practices concerning the connection between education and science. Brain research has opened a new era of thought regarding teaching and learning. As education has left the industrial era model of teaching, it has to build a foundation for a new Informational era of learning, and I see that happening, but at the expense of other important skill categories that ensure social development, sensory integration, self-expression, and interpersonal communication.

It is possible, by following a brain-compatible curriculum, to integrate technology, multiple intelligences, and different learning styles, but it would help teachers a lot if they were taught the skills they need to do this before entering the classroom.

Having knowledge of the hidden disability, vision dysfunction, was so important to my teaching career that it deserves to be shared by educators all over the world. As I reflect on the difference that this knowledge made, I can only suppose that knowledge of other little-known conditions like the retention of neonatal or primitive reflexes (tonic neck syndromes), auditory processing disorder, and sensory processing disorder, would have made even more of a positive impact on my teaching strategies. If I had been better prepared to recognize existing, debilitating conditions of the child, I would have been made more aware of the whole child and how to address his needs.

CHAPTER 18
The Big Ideas

*T*HE BIG POINT IS THAT WITH THE MIRACLE OF conception in the womb, a whole child, complete with a spirit, mind, body, and emotions, is developing. This development is purposeful, simultaneous, chronological, and interconnected. Just weeks after conception, the child is beginning to respond to and make sense of his environment. The needs of the child have to be met by the mother or caregiver for the child to grow and develop the way it should to be prepared for life outside of the womb. The physical state of the child, which includes movement, sensory stimulation, emotional connections, and overall good health, command attention during the first dimension of learning. The blueprint is there; we just have to follow it in order to complete the construction of the whole child.

As with any form of nature, imperfections can occur. Sometimes the child is born with physical, mental, or emotional conditions that prove to be disheartening and difficult for parents and families. They don't reap the same rewards and joys that the average parent experiences. Very often milestones are delayed or never met and expected behaviors never witnessed.

I am basing this statement on my experiences with personal

friends who have had children with disabilities. Their journey has been colored with stress and heartbreaking experiences. In spite of all of their disappointments, they have been loving, strong, and amazing caregivers. They knew that no matter what, their child was a whole child with a mind, spirit, body, and emotions, maybe not the same as you, but the same in his need for love, caring, and understanding. Whether disabled or not, while in the home, the child learns how to make sense of her environment, how to navigate not only physically, but cognitively and emotionally. She is being prepared for life outside of the home. During this time, teaching your child emotional control and resiliency is going to be crucial to survival. Hopefully, she will be ready to leave the home with all the tools she needs to be successful in school, that third dimension of learning.

When the child enters school, it can be a rude awakening, just like leaving the womb and entering the outside world. The child has to adjust and learn how to make sense of his new environment. He or she has to learn how to communicate with teachers as well as peers. In addition to all these new responsibilities, he or she has to learn new things like reading, writing, and arithmetic, just to name a few. Experiencing the first days of school can be traumatizing for some children. Learning can be hijacked by emotions. Parents and teachers need to be aware of this so they can provide the support and nurturing that these children need. During this period of learning and development, the emotional control strategies and the attitude of resiliency that the learned in the home take on a new meaning. Becoming a truly social being takes lots of time and effort. Some never accomplish that task. Just saying.

The whole child enters the third dimension of learning with unique characteristics, cognitively, physically, and emotionally. He or she comes with a learning style and at least one dominant intelligence that have to be identified correctly. He or she uses his or her senses for making meaning out of the environment. If any of these senses are impacted by the slightest dysfunction, learning becomes more difficult, especially if not detected by the teacher early on.

All teachers should be taught that certain conditions exist that are capable of destroying children's chances of reaching their full academic potential. The average child who suffers from one of these conditions too often has one choice, which is to make the best of the situation. Children don't know that they are being affected by vision dysfunction or asymmetrical tonic neck syndrome; they only feel that something is wrong with them. Slowly but surely, they become defeated and lose all self-confidence. Most unfortunately, the teacher doesn't know either, so she will never be able to reach or understand that whole child.

Teachers have to be informed to recognize the symptoms of dysfunctions and given the tools to make appropriate recommendations as well as accommodations in the classroom. After all, exercises designed to help children with deficits accomplish that goal, while at the same time making children that don't have them stronger. Teachers, I know that you are saying to yourself, "Please, get real. With all the stuff we have to do now, that's impossible!" Well, you would be surprised at how easy it is to include activities in the classroom that support and address the needs of children with hidden disabilities. Every teacher should be required to take at least one semester class of occupational therapy, so that they can become familiar with the many developmental issues that affect so many of our students. These hidden conditions affect the child physically, mentally, emotionally, and socially.

Following the blueprint of brain development can help with organizing and prioritizing activities. Just as the area of emotions is in the center of the brain, emotional engagement should be at the core of classroom activities. Curricular development, which is informed by the knowledge that children learn better when they are having fun, is especially beneficial to children with disabilities, hidden or not.

Let us not forget the plight of the teacher, who wants to do his or her very best and knows what needs to be done, but whose hands are tied. In some school districts, teachers are penalized if their classes' test scores don't meet the set standards. Their evaluations are based on classroom observations and test results. In some states, if teachers get a couple of poor evaluations as a result of poor test performance, they can actually lose their jobs. Can you imagine how it must feel to know that your teaching will be judged and your future will be determined by circumstances beyond your control? Of course, I guess you could say "That's life," *if you're not a teacher*, but you have to remember that these teachers are considered to be in charge of a situation that is not controllable by them. They are being held responsible for each child's extenuating circumstances, which is just not fair.

Let's talk about the students. Just as students can feel their teacher's enthusiasm, they can also feel that teacher's frustration. Actually, there is as much stress put on students as there is put on teachers. Not only do students have to worry about the test itself, but they also worry about the plight of their teachers, especially the ones they love. This kind of negative stress only serves to create negative results. Science has informed us that when a person is under stress, cortisol, a chemical produced by the adrenal glands, is released and interferes with memory retrieval. Nobody needs that, especially during a life-altering test. Once again, educators and policy-makers need to acknowledge the scientific findings that are supportive of how the brain works.

My advice to teachers and administrators would be to make testing as much fun as possible. Life has informed us that attitude is everything. Knowing this, when I was in the classroom during the era of the first Ohio State Proficiency Exams, I decided that the attitudes toward testing had to be adjusted, so I solicited the help of a grocery store to provide free snacks for all the students who were being tested. If the store had refused my request, guess what? Like most teachers, I would have bought the snacks myself. Once the students heard about the food, their whole attitude changed from doom and gloom to great expectations. I told them that we could do stretches and yoga during the breaks. Most of them had never heard of yoga, but that didn't matter because it was the novelty of it all that got them excited about test time. Once their attitudes were on a more positive note, I began to tell them with as much enthusiasm as I could muster up that they would do great on the test as long as they did their very best. I would let them know that I was not worried. Of course, that was easy for me because at that time, my job didn't depend on test results.

There are lots of ways to get your class excited, but the easiest way is to introduce food of any kind. You could even allow them to bring in their own snacks. Maybe you or they could bring in music to play after testing. Have them make commercials about how great the tests are and how great their class is. Take pictures of the school's "greatest" class and post them in the classroom or even the hall. The point is, a change in attitudes can make a difference in scores.

Testing, in and of itself, is not automatically a bad thing. It can be very beneficial when used properly. Some form of the standardized testing should continue, but only if it is diagnostic and prescriptive in nature. The purpose it serves should be based on the academic needs of the child. I know it's unreasonable to think that testing will go away, because it does serve a purpose. However, it is not unreasonable for parents, teachers, administrators, and anyone with intelligence to "draw a line in the sand" and let the powers that be know that enough is enough. It's time for *punitive* testing to go away.

Great, so now we have trained all of our teachers and administrators to appreciate the importance of emotional engagement, to recognize possible hidden disabilities and act accordingly by including more brain-compatible classroom activities, and to accept and teach the whole child, but what about the training of the politicians who make the laws that govern our schools? The guidelines demand so much time to be spent on test preparation that there just seems to be no time available for social interaction or fun-filled activities. Who will inform the lawmakers about the importance of educational curricula that, instead of centering on testing, center on the development of the whole child?

We must find a way to influence educators as well as politicians. They must begin to acknowledge and appreciate the findings that science has to offer, as well as the interconnectedness of the mind, body, and spirit, and the mental, physical, and emotional states of the child. They need to embrace the rationale for teaching to those individual parts as one entity, the whole child. They need to acknowledge that testing just one or two intelligences and using those results to determine a child's lifelong identity is neither fair nor acceptable. Once that begins to take place on a wide scale, parents, teachers, and administrators, also known as the silent majority, have to speak as one voice. This voice has to be loud enough to reach the ears, minds, and hearts of the politicians who regulate our school programs from afar.

Wake up, educators and politicians! We are all in this together; "this" refers to the life of a world society that includes children, adults, the transgender, men, women, girls, boys, and all religions and ethnicities. When we are not informed about the dimensions of the whole child, clueless as to some of the conditions negatively affecting the academic and social growth of the child, then we are unequipped to teach in a way that can ensure every child's optimal success.

When the voice of our society's silent majority can bring about the emotional engagement of our lawmakers, we will see change, and our schools will finally do a much better job with fulfilling their obligation to our future. We have a blueprint; now let's follow it to make sure that the construction of the whole child is just what it needs to be.

GLOSSARY OF TERMS

Asymmetrical Tonic Neck Reflex: a primitive reflex found in newborn humans. Should disappear one month after birth.

Auditory Processing Disorder: A hearing problem that occurs when something interferes with the way the brain recognizes and interprets sounds, mainly speech.

Brain Compatible Learning: Learning in an environment that relates to how the brain functions, receiving, perceiving, and retrieving information at an optimal level.

Brain Gym: Trade name for educational kinesiology, which is a program that provides exercises that promote academic learning.

Enteric Nervous System: A main part of the nervous system influenced by emotions, where neurons (brain cells) are found in the throat, esophagus, stomach, and intestines.

Epigenetics: The study of anything other than DNA that influences gene expression and the development of an organism.

Fetal Age: Age determined by time of conception, two weeks less than gestational age.

Gender Identification: Distress experienced by an individual as a result of the sex and gender assigned to them at birth.

Gestational Age: The age of the pregnancy from the date of the last normal menstrual period.

Haptics: The process of identifying objects through touch.

Multiple Intelligences: A theory developed in 1983 by Howard Gardner that recognizes at least eight intelligences that account for a wide range of human potential.

Retained Primitive Reflexes: Primitive reflexes that remain past the first year of life outside the womb and interfere with social, academic, and motor learning. Autistic children as well as children with developmental disorders are known to have retained primitive reflexes.

Sensory Processing Disorder: Dysfunction in one or more of the sensory processing systems: auditory (hearing), gustatory (taste), olfactory (smell), proprioceptive (position in space), tactile (touch), vestibular (balance), and vision (sight).

Vision Dysfunction: Less-obvious vision problems related to the way the brain processes visual information, often limits child's ability to learn.

REFERENCES

American Optometric Association, (2016). Retrieved from
http://www.aoa.org/newsroom/the 21stcenturychild-increased-
technology-use-may-lead- to-future-eye-health-and-vision-issues?

Auditory Processing Disorder, (2014). Retrieved from
http://www.kidshealth.org/en/parents/central-auditory.html

Ayers, J. (1991). *Sensory Integration and learning disorders*. Los
Angeles, CA: Western Psychological Services.

Baby Presence, (2012). Proprioception. Retrieved from
https://babypresence.wordpress.com/2012/08/23/
proprioception/

Balance and Motion: Why Kids Like to Swing, Sway, Bounce
and Rock, (2016). Retrieved from http://www.gooeybrains.com

Barnard, N. D. (2007). Dr. Neal Barnard's Program for Reversing
Diabetes. New York, NY: Neal D. Bernard, MD

Billis, T. (2016). Understanding Auditory Processing Disorders in
Children.
Retrieved from http://www.asha.org/public/hearing/
understanding-Auditory-Processing-Disorders-In-Children/

Birnholz, J., Stephens, J. C., & Faria, M. (1978). Fetal movement
patterns using ultra sound. Retrieved from
http://www.ncbl.nlm.nih.gov/pubmed/415565

Blythe, S. (2009). Attention, Balance, and Coordination: the ABC's of Learning Success. Hoboken, N J: Wiley Publishers.

Bloomberg, H. (2015). Rhythmic movement training. Retrieved from http://www.bloombergrmt.com/rhythmic-movement-training.

Blog Epic Health Services, (2015). Retained primitive reflexes: causes and common Types and how pediatric therapy can help. Retrieved from http://www.blog.epichealthservices.com/retained-primitive-reflexes-causes-and-common-types-pediatric-therapy/

Busnel, M.C., Granier-Deferre.C, & Lecanuet, J.P. (1992). Perceptual Development : visual, auditory and speech perception in infancy. Retrieved from http://www.birthpsychology.com

Carey, N. (2012). *The Epigenetics Revolution: How Modern Biology Is Rewriting Our Understanding of Genetics, Disease and Inheritance.* New York, NY: Columbia University Press

Chamberlain, D. (2013). *Windows to the Womb: Revealing the Conscious Baby from Conception to Birth.* Berkley, CA: North Atlantic Books.

Childhood 101, (2016). Managing big emotions: take five breathing exercises. Retrieved from http://www.childhood101.com/2015/04/take-5-breathing-exercise/.

Daley, M. (2014). Hindsight is 20'20/20: protect your eyes from digital devices. Retrieved from http://www.thevisioncouncil.org

Damasio, A. R. (1994). *Descartes's error: emotion, reason, and the human brain. New York: Hayrer Collins.*

Dennison, P. and Dennison, G. (1987, revised 2010). Brain Gym: Teacher's Edition. Ventura, CA: EDu-Kinesthetics, Inc.

Developmental milestones: hearing, (2016). Retrieved from
http://www.babycentre.co.uk/96509/developmental.
milestones-hearing

Educational Psychology Services (2011). Helping children with auditory processing difficulties.
Retrieved from www.moray.gov.uk/downloads/file77541.pdf

Evans, J. (2013). Recognizing sensory processing disorders.
Retrieved from
http://www.janetlansbury.com/2013/09/recognizing-sensor
y-processing-disorders-spd-guest-post-by-jonathan-evans

Facts are Facts (2017). ADD/ADHD. Retrieved from
https://www.facts-are-facts.com/newsadd-adhd#.WPpNJtLyu70

Family Policy Institute (2016). Washington Schools to teach gender
identity curriculum in kindergarten. Retrieved from
http://www.fpiw.org/blog/2016/o6/o2/washington-schools-t
o-teach-gender=identity-curriculum-in-kindergarten/

Fetal development week by week, (2016). Retrieved from
http://www.babycentre.com.uk/pregnancy-week-by-week

Gallaway, M. (2010. The need for better school vision screening:
The use of VERA Vision screening in a community setting. The
journal of optometry and vision development, 41(4):232–39.
Gallop, S. (2016). Developmental/functional vision checklist.
Retrieved from
http://www.vision-therapy-pa.com/behavioral-optometry/
functional-vision-checklist.html

Gardner, H. (1965). *Frames of Mind: The Theory of Multiple
Intelligences*. New York. Basic Books.

Gavin, M. L. (2014). Auditory processing disorder special needs
fact sheet, Retrieved from http://www.hopkinsallchildren.org/
patients-families/healthdoc/auditory-processing-disorder-specia
l-needs-factshe?=21072

Goleman, D. (1996). *Emotional Intelligence: Why It Can Matter More than IQ*. New York: Bantam Books

Gravens, S. & Brown, J. (2008). Sensory Development in the Fetus, Neonate, and infant. Retrieved from http://www.nainr.com/gravens

Greene, A (2009). Raising Baby Greene: *The Earth Friendly Guide to Pregnancy, Children and Baby Care*. San Francisco: Wiley Publishers

Greutman, H. (2014). *How the Vestibular System Affects Your Child's Behavior*.
Retrieved from http:www.growinghandsonkids.com

Hannaford, C. (1995). *Smart Moves*. Arlington, VA: Great Oceans

Hopson, J.L., (2016). Your baby can feel, dream, and even listen to Mozart In the womb. Retrieved from http://www.psychologytoday.com/articles/199809/fetal-psychology/

Hughes, V, (2014). Epigenetics: The Sins of the Father. Retrieved from http://www.nature.com/news/epigenetics-the-sins-of-the-father

Hutchinson, A. (2016). Dehydration and cognitive function. Retrieved from www.runnersworld.com/sweet-science/dehydration-and cognitive-function

Hyman, M. (2008).Functional Wellness, Part 2: Hormones and Inflammation.
Retrieved from http://www.experiencelife.com/article/functional-wellness-part-2-hormones-and-inflammation/

Jeanie, (2009).What causes SPD. Retrieved from www.sensory.processing-Disorder.com/what-causes-spd.html

Jensen, E. (2000). *Brain-Based Learning*. San Diego, CA: The Brain Store

Jensen, E. (2000). *Amazing Brain Facts*. USA: Eric Jensen

Jensen, E. (2000). *Different Brains, Different Learners*: San Diego, CA: The Brain Store

Jensen, E. (2008*). Learning with the Body in Mind*. San Diego, CA: The Brain Store

Kovalik, S. (2001). Brain Compatible Learning through ITL. Retrieved from *http://www,.Kovalik.com*

Kranowitz, C. (2005). *The Out-of-Sync Child: Recognizing and Coping with Sensory Processing Disorder*. New York: Penguin Books

Latavia, C. (2016). Developing baby's 5 senses. Retrieved from http://www.parenting.com/article/developing-Baby's-5-Senses

LeDoux, J. (1996). *The Emotional Brain*. New York: Simon & Schuster

Loud noises during pregnancy. (2016). Retrieved from http://www.whattoexpect.com/pregnancy/ask-heidi/loud-noises.aspx

Littlejohn, M. (2011). How brain behavior works from conception to adulthood. Retrieved from http://www.spiritualbirth.com

Mandal, A. (2016). Causes of gender dysphoria. Retrieved from http://www.news-medical.net/health/causes-of-gender-Dysphoria.aspx

Manoff, (2013). An epidemic of absence: a new way of understanding allergies and autoimmune diseases. Retrieved from http://www.westonaprice.org/book-reviews/an-epidemic-of-disease-by-moises-velasquez-manoff

Mastrangelo, J. (2014). When does a baby develop gender? Retrieved from www.livestrong.com/article/231357/-when-does-a-baby-develop-gender/

Melillo, R. (2009). *Disconnected Kids*. New York, NY: Penguin Group.

Melillo, R. (2016). Brain balance exercises for Retained Primitive Reflexes.
Retrieved from http://www.drrobertmelillo.com/2016/03/1 8/5exercises-inhibit-primitive/reflexes

Mercola, (2001). Insulin Diet. Retrieved from http://www.articles.mercola.com/sites/articles/ archive/2001/07/14/insulin-part-one-aspx

Moybray, L. (2010). Primitive reflex training: visual dynamix. Retrieved from http://www.visiontherapyathome.com

Pert, C. (1997). *Molecules of Emotion.* New York: Scribner

Rajeev, L. (2015). Brain development in the fetus. Retrieved from http://www.buzzle.com/articles/brain-development-in-fetus

Sexual orientation and gender identity 101. (2016). Retrieved from http://www.uua.org/lgbtq/identity

Shymansky, J. & Wesson, K. (2012). Brain-Sight: Can Touch Allow Us to See Better Than Sight. Retrieved from http:// www.brainworldmagazine.com/brain-sight-can-touch-allow-u s-to- see-better-than-sight

Sousa, D. (2001). *How the Brain Learns* (2nd ed.). Thousand Oaks, CA: Corwin.

Stanbury, J. (2016). Sensory integration disorder: the hidden handicap.
Retrieved from http://www.battlegrondhealingarts.com/articles/ sensory-Integration-disorder-the-hidden-handicap

Streff, J. & Gunderson, E. (2004). *Childhood Learning: Journey or Race.*

Teele, S. (2009). *Rainbows of Intelligence: Exploring How Students Learn.* Thousand Oaks: Corwin

10 Ways to Balance Blood Sugar Naturally. (2014). Retrieved from http://www.empoweredsustenance.com/ balance-blood-sugar-naturally/

The Insulin/Cancer connection. (2016). Retrieved from http://www.lifeextension.com/Magazine/2016/ The-Insulin-Cancer-Connection/Page-01

The 21st Century child: increased technology use may lead to future eye health and vision issues. (2016). Retrieved from http://www.aoa.org/newsroom/the 21stcenturychild-increased-use-may-lead-to-future-eye-health-and-vision-issues?

The learning clinic, (2016). Reflexes. Retrieved from http://www.thelearningclinic.ie/index.php/programs/movement-therapy/reflexes/

The vision council, (2016). Signs and symptoms of learning related vision problems. Retrieved from http://www.covd.org

Understood Team,(2016). Understanding auditory Processing Disorder. Retrieved from http://www.understood.org/en/learning-attention-issues/child-learning-disabilities/auditory-processing-disorder/understanding-auditory-processing-disorder.

Weinhold, B. (2006). Epigenetics: the science of change. Retrieved from http://www.ncbl,nim.nih.gov-NCBL-Literature-Pubmedcentral(pmc)

What babies learn in the womb, (2015). Retrieved from http://www.parenting.com/article/what-babies-learn-in-the-womb

Wikipedia, (2016). Ted Kaczynski. Retrieved from https://en.wikipedia.org/wiki/Ted_Kaczynski

Figures

Figure 1.2: Week 9, embryo becomes official fetus.

Retrieved from http://www.thinkstock.com

Figure1.3: Week 12 marks the end of the first trimester.

Retrieved from http://www.thinkstock.com

Figure 1.4: Fetus positioned in womb, end of first trimester.

Retrieved from http://www.thinkstock.com

Figure 1.5: Week 16, baby reaches and tugs on umbilical cord.

Retrieved from http://www.thinkstock.com

Figure1.6: Week 20, sensory perception is developing rapidly.

Retrieved from http://www.thinkstock.com.

Figure 1.7; Week 24, brain now regulates all body functions, auditory and visual systems activated.

Figure 1.8: End of second trimester.

Retrieved from http://www.thinkstock.com

Figure 1.9: Week 29 marks beginning of third trimester.

Retrieved from http://www.thinkstock.com

Figure 2.1: The brainstem.

Retrieved from http://www.thinkstock.com

Figure 2.2: The cerebrum.

Retrieved from http://www.thinkstock.com

Figure 2.3: The limbic system.

Retrieved from http://www.thinkstock.com

Figure 2.4: The cerebral cortex.

Retrieved from http:www.thinkstock.com

Figure 2.5: Lobes of the cerebral cortex.

Retrieved from http://www.thinkstock.com

Figure 4.1; Children's brains ruled by technology.

Retrieved from http://www.thinkstock.com

Figure 4.2: Simple vision screening is not enough.

Retrieved from http://www.brainabdeyeconnection.com.

Figure 6.1: Sensory experiences.
Retrieved from http://www.thinkstock.com

Figure 7.1: Image for primitive reflex (Moro reflex)
Illustrated by Brenda Hunter

Figure 7.2: Image for primitive reflex (tonic neck reflex)
Illustrated by Brenda Hunter

Figures 7.3–7.8: Tests for retained primitive reflexes.
Illustrated by Matt Brady

Figure 9.1: A self-regulation technique.
Retrieved from http://www.thinkstock.com

Figure 9.2: Conflict Resolution
Retrieved from http://www.thinkstock.com

Figure 10.1: Brain Gym (PACE) moves.
Dennison, P. & Dennison, G. (2010). *Brain Gym. Ventura, CA: EDu-Kinesthetics,Inc.*

Figure 10.2: Examples of Onomatopoeia
Illustrated by Brenda Hunter

Figure 12.1: Everything technology.
Retrieved from http://www.thinkstock.com

Figure 12.2: Vision testing: Snellen chart.
Retrieved from http://www.thinkstock.com.

Figure 14.1: Sensory processing disorder
Retrieved from http//www.cornerstonepediatriccenter.com

Figure 16.1: Sugar addiction starts way too early.
Illustrated by Brenda Hunter, (2017)

Figure 17.1: Action screen shot of Larry Fitzgerald.
Retrieved from http://www.gettyimages.com

ABOUT THE AUTHOR

DR. CAROLYN NOOKS TEAGUE holds a doctorate in educational leadership with a focus on brain-compatible-learning. She is a retired elementary teacher who taught for thirty years combined in both public and private schools of Cincinnati and Chicago. In addition to being an elementary teacher, Dr. Teague served as the director of a preschool as well as an adjunct college professor. She was trained as a vision therapist under Dr. David Muth, a behavioral optometrist of Cincinnati, Ohio, and practiced vision therapy in the classroom as well as private practice.

Dr. Teague was introduced to the hidden disability of vision dysfunction and the therapy used to treat it while teaching in Chicago with the Woodlawn Experimental Schools project. Training for this program was provided by behavioral optometrists, Dr. Robert Johnson and Dr. Henry Moore, directors of the Plano Child Development Center. This experience opened her eyes to the many dimensions of children and how they learn. During this time, she left the classroom to work as an educational consultant for Chicago's Center for Inner City Studies. While there, she wrote programs on the psycholinguistic approach to learning and consulted with parents, teachers, and students in the public schools of Topeka, Kansas, Los Angeles, and Chicago on how to use this program to increase student academic success.

When her tenure at the Center for Inner City Studies was completed, Dr. Teague became a reading consultant with Harcourt Brace Jovanovich Publishers. After five years of consulting for Harcourt, Dr. Teague got married and moved back to her hometown, Cincinnati. There she had two children and returned to the classroom as a fourth-grade teacher.

The daughter of an elementary teacher, Dr. Teague, was destined to follow suit. Her mother taught her the importance of dealing with the whole child and accepting him unconditionally. While visiting St. Petersburg, Russia, for an international science conference, she had the opportunity to observe the broad meaning of teaching the whole child in a brain-compatible curriculum in action; she knew that she had work to do. She wanted to learn more, and she did. Her passion for her students' success, in addition to her rich experiences, and faith in God, have given her a voice.

Dr. Teague now resides in Cincinnati, Ohio. She is a grandmother and an avid researcher. She loves swimming, line dancing, and movies. She is now writing another book about the depth and breadth of her African American/Native American ancestry.